Hybrid Clouds
Complete Self-Assessment Guide

C000053039

The guidance in this Self-Assessment is based c
practices and standards in business process arcı...ᴄᴄ.ᴜɾᴇ, design and
quality management. The guidance is also based on the professional
judgment of the individual collaborators listed in the Acknowledgments.

Notice of rights

Trademarks

Many of the designations used by manufacturers and sellers to
distinguish their products are claimed as trademarks. Where those
designations appear in this book, and the publisher was aware of a
trademark claim, the designations appear as requested by the owner
of the trademark. All other product names and services identified
throughout this book are used in editorial fashion only and for the
benefit of such companies with no intention of infringement of the
trademark. No such use, or the use of any trade name, is intended to
convey endorsement or other affiliation with this book.

Copyright © by The Art of Service
http://theartofservice.com
service@theartofservice.com

Table of Contents

About The Art of Service

The Art of Service, Business Process Architects since 2000, is dedicated to helping stakeholders achieve excellence.

Defining, designing, creating, and implementing a process to solve a stakeholders challenge or meet an objective is the most valuable role… In EVERY group, company, organization and department.

Unless you're talking a one-time, single-use project, there should be a process. Whether that process is managed and implemented by humans, AI, or a combination of the two, it needs to be designed by someone with a complex enough perspective to ask the right questions.

Someone capable of asking the right questions and step back and say, 'What are we really trying to accomplish here? And is there a different way to look at it?'

With The Art of Service's Standard Requirements Self-Assessments, we empower people who can do just that — whether their title is marketer, entrepreneur, manager, salesperson, consultant, Business Process Manager, executive assistant, IT Manager, CIO etc... —they are the people who rule the future. They are people who watch the process as it happens, and ask the right questions to make the process work better.

Contact us when you need any support with this Self-Assessment and any help with templates, blue-prints and examples of standard documents you might need:

http://theartofservice.com
service@theartofservice.com

Included Resources - how to access

Included with your purchase of the book is the Hybrid Clouds

Self-Assessment Spreadsheet Dashboard which contains all questions and Self-Assessment areas and auto-generates insights, graphs, and project RACI planning - all with examples to get you started right away.

How? Simply send an email to
access@theartofservice.com
with this books' title in the subject to get the Hybrid Clouds Self Assessment Tool right away.

You will receive the following contents with New and Updated specific criteria:

- The latest quick edition of the book in PDF

- The latest complete edition of the book in PDF, which criteria correspond to the criteria in...

- The Self-Assessment Excel Dashboard, and...

- Example pre-filled Self-Assessment Excel Dashboard to get familiar with results generation

- In-depth specific Checklists covering the topic

- Project management checklists and templates to assist with implementation

INCLUDES LIFETIME SELF ASSESSMENT UPDATES

Every self assessment comes with Lifetime Updates and Lifetime Free Updated Books. Lifetime Updates is an industry-first feature which allows you to receive verified self assessment updates, ensuring you always have the most accurate information at your fingertips.

Get it now- you will be glad you did - do it now, before you forget.

Send an email to **access@theartofservice.com** with this books' title in the subject to get the Hybrid Clouds Self Assessment Tool right away.

Purpose of this Self-Assessment

This Self-Assessment has been developed to improve understanding of the requirements and elements of Hybrid Clouds, based on best practices and standards in business process architecture, design and quality management.

It is designed to allow for a rapid Self-Assessment to determine how closely existing management practices and procedures correspond to the elements of the Self-Assessment.

The criteria of requirements and elements of Hybrid Clouds have been rephrased in the format of a Self-Assessment questionnaire, with a seven-criterion scoring system, as explained in this document.

In this format, even with limited background knowledge of Hybrid Clouds, a manager can quickly review existing operations to determine how they measure up to the standards. This in turn can serve as the starting point of a 'gap analysis' to identify management tools or system elements that might usefully be implemented in the organization to help improve overall performance.

How to use the Self-Assessment

On the following pages are a series of questions to identify to what extent your Hybrid Clouds initiative is complete in comparison to the requirements set in standards.

To facilitate answering the questions, there is a space in front of each question to enter a score on a scale of '1' to '5'.

1 Strongly Disagree

2 Disagree

3 Neutral

4 Agree

5 Strongly Agree

Read the question and rate it with the following in front of mind:

'In my belief,
the answer to this question is clearly defined'.

There are two ways in which you can choose to interpret this statement;
1. how aware are you that the answer to the question is clearly defined
2. for more in-depth analysis you can choose to gather evidence and confirm the answer to the question. This obviously will take more time, most Self-Assessment users opt for the first way to interpret the question and dig deeper later on based on the outcome of the overall Self-Assessment.

A score of '1' would mean that the answer is not clear at all, where a '5' would mean the answer is crystal clear and defined. Leave emtpy when the question is not applicable or you don't want to answer it, you can skip it without affecting your score. Write your score in the space provided.

After you have responded to all the appropriate statements in each section, compute your average score for that section, using the formula provided, and round to the nearest tenth. Then transfer to the corresponding spoke in the Hybrid Clouds Scorecard on the second next page of the Self-Assessment.

Your completed Hybrid Clouds Scorecard will give you a clear presentation of which Hybrid Clouds areas need attention.

Hybrid Clouds
Scorecard Example

Example of how the finalized Scorecard can look like:

Hybrid Clouds
Scorecard

Your Scores:

BEGINNING OF THE SELF-ASSESSMENT:

CRITERION #1: RECOGNIZE

INTENT: Be aware of the need for change. Recognize that there is an unfavorable variation, problem or symptom.

In my belief, the answer to this question is clearly defined:

5 Strongly Agree

4 Agree

3 Neutral

2 Disagree

1 Strongly Disagree

1. Why the need?
<--- Score

2. What creative shifts do you need to take?
<--- Score

3. Will hybrid clouds deliverables need to be tested and, if so, by whom?
<--- Score

4. Are losses recognized in a timely manner?
<--- Score

5. What prevents you from making the changes you know will make you a more effective hybrid clouds leader?
<--- Score

6. When a hybrid clouds manager recognizes a problem, what options are available?
<--- Score

7. Who should resolve the hybrid clouds issues?
<--- Score

8. Do you need to avoid or amend any hybrid clouds activities?
<--- Score

9. What are the stakeholder objectives to be achieved with hybrid clouds?
<--- Score

10. How does it fit into your organizational needs and tasks?
<--- Score

11. What are your needs in relation to hybrid clouds skills, labor, equipment, and markets?
<--- Score

12. For your hybrid clouds project, identify and describe the business environment, is there more than one layer to the business environment?
<--- Score

13. Looking at each person individually – does every one have the qualities which are needed to work in this group?
<--- Score

14. Are there any specific expectations or concerns about the hybrid clouds team, hybrid clouds itself?
<--- Score

15. What vendors make products that address the hybrid clouds needs?
<--- Score

16. Is it needed?
<--- Score

17. What is the extent or complexity of the hybrid clouds problem?
<--- Score

18. What hybrid clouds events should you attend?
<--- Score

19. What needs to be done?
<--- Score

20. As a sponsor, customer or management, how important is it to meet goals, objectives?
<--- Score

21. How much are sponsors, customers, partners, stakeholders involved in hybrid clouds? In other words, what are the risks, if hybrid clouds does not deliver successfully?
<--- Score

22. What is the smallest subset of the problem you can usefully solve?
<--- Score

23. What does hybrid clouds success mean to the stakeholders?
<--- Score

24. What hybrid clouds coordination do you need?
<--- Score

25. To what extent does each concerned units management team recognize hybrid clouds as an effective investment?
<--- Score

26. How are training requirements identified?
<--- Score

27. How do you identify the kinds of information that you will need?
<--- Score

28. Which issues are too important to ignore?
<--- Score

29. Are you dealing with any of the same issues today as yesterday? What can you do about this?
<--- Score

30. Whom do you really need or want to serve?
<--- Score

31. Who are your key stakeholders who need to sign off?

<--- Score

32. Would you recognize a threat from the inside?
<--- Score

33. Have you identified your hybrid clouds key performance indicators?
<--- Score

34. What hybrid clouds problem should be solved?
<--- Score

35. How do you recognize an objection?
<--- Score

36. Who defines the rules in relation to any given issue?
<--- Score

37. What would happen if hybrid clouds weren't done?
<--- Score

38. What information do users need?
<--- Score

39. Where do you need to exercise leadership?
<--- Score

40. Is it clear when you think of the day ahead of you what activities and tasks you need to complete?
<--- Score

41. Are there recognized hybrid clouds problems?
<--- Score

42. Will new equipment/products be required to facilitate hybrid clouds delivery, for example is new software needed?
<--- Score

43. Who needs what information?
<--- Score

44. Are your goals realistic? Do you need to redefine your problem? Perhaps the problem has changed or maybe you have reached your goal and need to set a new one?
<--- Score

45. Is the quality assurance team identified?
<--- Score

46. Who needs to know?
<--- Score

47. Did you miss any major hybrid clouds issues?
<--- Score

48. Do you recognize hybrid clouds achievements?
<--- Score

49. Why is this needed?
<--- Score

50. Do you know what you need to know about hybrid clouds?
<--- Score

51. Are controls defined to recognize and contain problems?
<--- Score

52. To what extent would your organization benefit from being recognized as a award recipient?
<--- Score

53. Will it solve real problems?
<--- Score

54. What are the clients issues and concerns?
<--- Score

55. Consider your own hybrid clouds project, what types of organizational problems do you think might be causing or affecting your problem, based on the work done so far?
<--- Score

56. How do you assess your hybrid clouds workforce capability and capacity needs, including skills, competencies, and staffing levels?
<--- Score

57. Who else hopes to benefit from it?
<--- Score

58. Is the need for organizational change recognized?
<--- Score

59. What is the problem or issue?
<--- Score

60. What is the hybrid clouds problem definition? What do you need to resolve?
<--- Score

61. Can management personnel recognize the

monetary benefit of hybrid clouds?
<--- Score

62. What are the hybrid clouds resources needed?
<--- Score

63. Does your organization need more hybrid clouds education?
<--- Score

64. What is the recognized need?
<--- Score

65. Do you need different information or graphics?
<--- Score

66. How are the hybrid clouds's objectives aligned to the group's overall stakeholder strategy?
<--- Score

67. What are the expected benefits of hybrid clouds to the stakeholder?
<--- Score

68. Do you have/need 24-hour access to key personnel?
<--- Score

69. What situation(s) led to this hybrid clouds Self Assessment?
<--- Score

70. How do thorny interoperability issues play out in hybrid clouds?
<--- Score

71. How are you going to measure success?
<--- Score

72. Does the problem have ethical dimensions?
<--- Score

73. How can auditing be a preventative security measure?
<--- Score

74. Who needs to know about hybrid clouds?
<--- Score

75. Will a response program recognize when a crisis occurs and provide some level of response?
<--- Score

76. Where is training needed?
<--- Score

77. Are there regulatory / compliance issues?
<--- Score

78. Are employees recognized for desired behaviors?
<--- Score

79. How do you recognize an hybrid clouds objection?
<--- Score

80. Which needs are not included or involved?
<--- Score

81. Which information does the hybrid clouds business case need to include?
<--- Score

82. How many trainings, in total, are needed?
<--- Score

83. What should be considered when identifying available resources, constraints, and deadlines?
<--- Score

84. Are problem definition and motivation clearly presented?
<--- Score

85. What are the minority interests and what amount of minority interests can be recognized?
<--- Score

86. Think about the people you identified for your hybrid clouds project and the project responsibilities you would assign to them, what kind of training do you think they would need to perform these responsibilities effectively?
<--- Score

87. Does hybrid clouds create potential expectations in other areas that need to be recognized and considered?
<--- Score

88. How do you take a forward-looking perspective in identifying hybrid clouds research related to market response and models?
<--- Score

89. What extra resources will you need?
<--- Score

90. What needs to stay?

<--- Score

91. What problems are you facing and how do you consider hybrid clouds will circumvent those obstacles?
<--- Score

92. What resources or support might you need?
<--- Score

93. Are employees recognized or rewarded for performance that demonstrates the highest levels of integrity?
<--- Score

94. Are there any revenue recognition issues?
<--- Score

95. What are the timeframes required to resolve each of the issues/problems?
<--- Score

96. What activities does the governance board need to consider?
<--- Score

97. How do you identify subcontractor relationships?
<--- Score

Add up total points for this section:
_ _ _ _ _ = Total points for this section

Divided by: _ _ _ _ _ _ (number of statements answered) = _ _ _ _ _ _
Average score for this section

Transfer your score to the hybrid clouds
Index at the beginning of the Self-
Assessment.

CRITERION #2: DEFINE:

INTENT: Formulate the stakeholder problem. Define the problem, needs and objectives.

In my belief, the answer to this question is clearly defined:

5 Strongly Agree

4 Agree

3 Neutral

2 Disagree

1 Strongly Disagree

1. Has your scope been defined?
<--- Score

2. What are the requirements for audit information?
<--- Score

3. When are meeting minutes sent out? Who is on the distribution list?
<--- Score

4. How will variation in the actual durations of each activity be dealt with to ensure that the expected hybrid clouds results are met?
<--- Score

5. Have all basic functions of hybrid clouds been defined?
<--- Score

6. How does the hybrid clouds manager ensure against scope creep?
<--- Score

7. Does the scope remain the same?
<--- Score

8. What is the scope?
<--- Score

9. The political context: who holds power?
<--- Score

10. When is the estimated completion date?
<--- Score

11. Have all of the relationships been defined properly?
<--- Score

12. Are there different segments of customers?
<--- Score

13. Is the work to date meeting requirements?
<--- Score

14. Is there a clear hybrid clouds case definition?
<--- Score

15. What are the Roles and Responsibilities for each team member and its leadership? Where is this documented?
<--- Score

16. Are audit criteria, scope, frequency and methods defined?
<--- Score

17. Is special hybrid clouds user knowledge required?
<--- Score

18. If substitutes have been appointed, have they been briefed on the hybrid clouds goals and received regular communications as to the progress to date?
<--- Score

19. Has the hybrid clouds work been fairly and/or equitably divided and delegated among team members who are qualified and capable to perform the work? Has everyone contributed?
<--- Score

20. Has a project plan, Gantt chart, or similar been developed/completed?
<--- Score

21. When is/was the hybrid clouds start date?
<--- Score

22. Are the hybrid clouds requirements complete?
<--- Score

23. What key stakeholder process output measure(s) does hybrid clouds leverage and how?
<--- Score

24. Is there any additional hybrid clouds definition of success?
<--- Score

25. Who is gathering information?
<--- Score

26. Has the improvement team collected the 'voice of the customer' (obtained feedback – qualitative and quantitative)?
<--- Score

27. Where can you gather more information?
<--- Score

28. What is the context?
<--- Score

29. Who approved the hybrid clouds scope?
<--- Score

30. What are the core elements of the hybrid clouds business case?
<--- Score

31. How do you build the right business case?
<--- Score

32. What sources do you use to gather information for a hybrid clouds study?
<--- Score

33. What system do you use for gathering hybrid clouds information?
<--- Score

34. What is the scope of the hybrid clouds work?
<--- Score

35. Is there a critical path to deliver hybrid clouds results?
<--- Score

36. What knowledge or experience is required?
<--- Score

37. Are accountability and ownership for hybrid clouds clearly defined?
<--- Score

38. What would be the goal or target for a hybrid clouds's improvement team?
<--- Score

39. What are (control) requirements for hybrid clouds Information?
<--- Score

40. Has anyone else (internal or external to the group) attempted to solve this problem or a similar one before? If so, what knowledge can be leveraged from these previous efforts?
<--- Score

41. What intelligence can you gather?
<--- Score

42. How do you hand over hybrid clouds context?

<--- Score

43. What is the definition of success?
<--- Score

44. Is it clearly defined in and to your organization what you do?
<--- Score

45. How can the value of hybrid clouds be defined?
<--- Score

46. What are the hybrid clouds tasks and definitions?
<--- Score

47. How do you think the partners involved in hybrid clouds would have defined success?
<--- Score

48. How and when will the baselines be defined?
<--- Score

49. Do the problem and goal statements meet the SMART criteria (specific, measurable, attainable, relevant, and time-bound)?
<--- Score

50. Are customer(s) identified and segmented according to their different needs and requirements?
<--- Score

51. What is the definition of hybrid clouds excellence?
<--- Score

52. Is the team equipped with available and reliable resources?

<--- Score

53. Does the team have regular meetings?
<--- Score

54. Has/have the customer(s) been identified?
<--- Score

55. Who are the hybrid clouds improvement team members, including Management Leads and Coaches?
<--- Score

56. What is a worst-case scenario for losses?
<--- Score

57. How will the hybrid clouds team and the group measure complete success of hybrid clouds?
<--- Score

58. Will team members regularly document their hybrid clouds work?
<--- Score

59. What are the hybrid clouds use cases?
<--- Score

60. What is out-of-scope initially?
<--- Score

61. Are roles and responsibilities formally defined?
<--- Score

62. Is there regularly 100% attendance at the team meetings? If not, have appointed substitutes attended to preserve cross-functionality and full

representation?

<--- Score

63. Are all requirements met?

<--- Score

64. How do you manage scope?

<--- Score

65. How do you catch hybrid clouds definition inconsistencies?

<--- Score

66. How do you manage changes in hybrid clouds requirements?

<--- Score

67. What happens if hybrid clouds's scope changes?

<--- Score

68. How do you keep key subject matter experts in the loop?

<--- Score

69. Is hybrid clouds currently on schedule according to the plan?

<--- Score

70. What customer feedback methods were used to solicit their input?

<--- Score

71. What is the scope of the hybrid clouds effort?

<--- Score

72. Do you have organizational privacy requirements?

<--- Score

73. Will team members perform hybrid clouds work when assigned and in a timely fashion?
<--- Score

74. What was the context?
<--- Score

75. What is in the scope and what is not in scope?
<--- Score

76. Scope of sensitive information?
<--- Score

77. How often are the team meetings?
<--- Score

78. Is hybrid clouds linked to key stakeholder goals and objectives?
<--- Score

79. What baselines are required to be defined and managed?
<--- Score

80. Who defines (or who defined) the rules and roles?
<--- Score

81. How have you defined all hybrid clouds requirements first?
<--- Score

82. Has everyone on the team, including the team leaders, been properly trained?
<--- Score

83. How do you manage unclear hybrid clouds requirements?

<--- Score

84. What scope to assess?

<--- Score

85. What is in scope?

<--- Score

86. Is the team adequately staffed with the desired cross-functionality? If not, what additional resources are available to the team?

<--- Score

87. Do you have a hybrid clouds success story or case study ready to tell and share?

<--- Score

88. Are resources adequate for the scope?

<--- Score

89. Do you all define hybrid clouds in the same way?

<--- Score

90. How do you gather hybrid clouds requirements?

<--- Score

91. How do you gather the stories?

<--- Score

92. Is the hybrid clouds scope manageable?

<--- Score

93. What sort of initial information to gather?

<--- Score

94. What information should you gather?
<--- Score

95. What are the dynamics of the communication plan?
<--- Score

96. Is data collected and displayed to better understand customer(s) critical needs and requirements.
<--- Score

97. Are different versions of process maps needed to account for the different types of inputs?
<--- Score

98. Is there a hybrid clouds management charter, including stakeholder case, problem and goal statements, scope, milestones, roles and responsibilities, communication plan?
<--- Score

99. Is the improvement team aware of the different versions of a process: what they think it is vs. what it actually is vs. what it should be vs. what it could be?
<--- Score

100. What specifically is the problem? Where does it occur? When does it occur? What is its extent?
<--- Score

101. Are task requirements clearly defined?
<--- Score

102. Is there a completed SIPOC representation, describing the Suppliers, Inputs, Process, Outputs, and Customers?
<--- Score

103. Why are you doing hybrid clouds and what is the scope?
<--- Score

104. Who is gathering hybrid clouds information?
<--- Score

105. What are the rough order estimates on cost savings/opportunities that hybrid clouds brings?
<--- Score

106. Is there a completed, verified, and validated high-level 'as is' (not 'should be' or 'could be') stakeholder process map?
<--- Score

107. How was the 'as is' process map developed, reviewed, verified and validated?
<--- Score

108. Has a team charter been developed and communicated?
<--- Score

109. Has a high-level 'as is' process map been completed, verified and validated?
<--- Score

110. In what way can you redefine the criteria of choice clients have in your category in your favor?
<--- Score

111. What information do you gather?
<--- Score

112. Are the hybrid clouds requirements testable?
<--- Score

113. Has a hybrid clouds requirement not been met?
<--- Score

114. How are consistent hybrid clouds definitions important?
<--- Score

115. Is hybrid clouds required?
<--- Score

116. What hybrid clouds requirements should be gathered?
<--- Score

117. Is the hybrid clouds scope complete and appropriately sized?
<--- Score

118. Is scope creep really all bad news?
<--- Score

119. What are the boundaries of the scope? What is in bounds and what is not? What is the start point? What is the stop point?
<--- Score

120. What hybrid clouds services do you require?
<--- Score

121. How did the hybrid clouds manager receive input to the development of a hybrid clouds improvement plan and the estimated completion dates/times of each activity?
<--- Score

122. What critical content must be communicated – who, what, when, where, and how?
<--- Score

123. How do you gather requirements?
<--- Score

124. Has the direction changed at all during the course of hybrid clouds? If so, when did it change and why?
<--- Score

125. How would you define hybrid clouds leadership?
<--- Score

126. What are the record-keeping requirements of hybrid clouds activities?
<--- Score

127. Are there any constraints known that bear on the ability to perform hybrid clouds work? How is the team addressing them?
<--- Score

128. What is out of scope?
<--- Score

129. What are the compelling stakeholder reasons for embarking on hybrid clouds?
<--- Score

130. What scope do you want your strategy to cover?
<--- Score

131. Is the current 'as is' process being followed? If not, what are the discrepancies?
<--- Score

132. Have specific policy objectives been defined?
<--- Score

133. How is the team tracking and documenting its work?
<--- Score

134. What defines best in class?
<--- Score

135. What gets examined?
<--- Score

136. Have the customer needs been translated into specific, measurable requirements? How?
<--- Score

137. What constraints exist that might impact the team?
<--- Score

Add up total points for this section:
_ _ _ _ _ = Total points for this section

Divided by: _ _ _ _ _ _ (number of statements answered) = _ _ _ _ _ _
Average score for this section

Transfer your score to the hybrid clouds
Index at the beginning of the Self-
Assessment.

CRITERION #3: MEASURE:

INTENT: Gather the correct data. Measure the current performance and evolution of the situation.

In my belief, the answer to this question is clearly defined:

5 Strongly Agree

4 Agree

3 Neutral

2 Disagree

1 Strongly Disagree

1. Are hybrid clouds vulnerabilities categorized and prioritized?
<--- Score

2. What are the costs of delaying hybrid clouds action?
<--- Score

3. When should you bother with diagrams?
<--- Score

4. What is the total cost related to deploying hybrid clouds, including any consulting or professional services?
<--- Score

5. Do you have any cost hybrid clouds limitation requirements?
<--- Score

6. Which measures and indicators matter?
<--- Score

7. How is progress measured?
<--- Score

8. How do you measure variability?
<--- Score

9. What are the hybrid clouds key cost drivers?
<--- Score

10. Have design-to-cost goals been established?
<--- Score

11. How do you quantify and qualify impacts?
<--- Score

12. What is the total fixed cost?
<--- Score

13. How can you measure hybrid clouds in a systematic way?
<--- Score

14. What are hidden hybrid clouds quality costs?

<--- Score

15. Do you have an issue in getting priority?
<--- Score

16. Is the solution cost-effective?
<--- Score

17. What does verifying compliance entail?
<--- Score

18. Do the benefits outweigh the costs?
<--- Score

19. Where is the cost?
<--- Score

20. Does the hybrid clouds task fit the client's priorities?
<--- Score

21. How will you measure success?
<--- Score

22. What evidence is there and what is measured?
<--- Score

23. Are indirect costs charged to the hybrid clouds program?
<--- Score

24. What can be used to verify compliance?
<--- Score

25. Why a hybrid clouds focus?
<--- Score

26. What methods are feasible and acceptable to estimate the impact of reforms?
<--- Score

27. Is there an opportunity to verify requirements?
<--- Score

28. What is measured? Why?
<--- Score

29. Which hybrid clouds impacts are significant?
<--- Score

30. What happens if cost savings do not materialize?
<--- Score

31. Does management have the right priorities among projects?
<--- Score

32. How do you measure success?
<--- Score

33. What details are required of the hybrid clouds cost structure?
<--- Score

34. How sensitive must the hybrid clouds strategy be to cost?
<--- Score

35. What are the types and number of measures to use?
<--- Score

36. How frequently do you verify your hybrid clouds strategy?
<--- Score

37. What does losing customers cost your organization?
<--- Score

38. What causes innovation to fail or succeed in your organization?
<--- Score

39. Do you aggressively reward and promote the people who have the biggest impact on creating excellent hybrid clouds services/products?
<--- Score

40. What is the hybrid clouds business impact?
<--- Score

41. When are costs are incurred?
<--- Score

42. Is the cost worth the hybrid clouds effort ?
<--- Score

43. Have you included everything in your hybrid clouds cost models?
<--- Score

44. What are allowable costs?
<--- Score

45. Who pays the cost?
<--- Score

46. What could cause you to change course?
<--- Score

47. What are your customers expectations and measures?
<--- Score

48. How will you measure your hybrid clouds effectiveness?
<--- Score

49. How long to keep data and how to manage retention costs?
<--- Score

50. How can you measure the performance?
<--- Score

51. Who should receive measurement reports?
<--- Score

52. Was a business case (cost/benefit) developed?
<--- Score

53. What is an unallowable cost?
<--- Score

54. What causes extra work or rework?
<--- Score

55. How can a hybrid clouds test verify your ideas or assumptions?
<--- Score

56. How do you verify if hybrid clouds is built right?
<--- Score

57. What are your primary costs, revenues, assets?
<--- Score

58. How will success or failure be measured?
<--- Score

59. What are your key hybrid clouds organizational performance measures, including key short and longer-term financial measures?
<--- Score

60. How will your organization measure success?
<--- Score

61. How to cause the change?
<--- Score

62. What does your operating model cost?
<--- Score

63. How can you reduce costs?
<--- Score

64. Which costs should be taken into account?
<--- Score

65. What potential environmental factors impact the hybrid clouds effort?
<--- Score

66. Are missed hybrid clouds opportunities costing your organization money?
<--- Score

67. What are the operational costs after hybrid clouds

deployment?
<--- Score

68. Who is involved in verifying compliance?
<--- Score

69. How do you verify hybrid clouds completeness and accuracy?
<--- Score

70. What do you measure and why?
<--- Score

71. Do you have a flow diagram of what happens?
<--- Score

72. How are measurements made?
<--- Score

73. Are you able to realize any cost savings?
<--- Score

74. How much does it cost?
<--- Score

75. How frequently do you track hybrid clouds measures?
<--- Score

76. What are the costs and benefits?
<--- Score

77. What are the strategic priorities for this year?
<--- Score

78. The approach of traditional hybrid clouds works

for detail complexity but is focused on a systematic approach rather than an understanding of the nature of systems themselves, what approach will permit your organization to deal with the kind of unpredictable emergent behaviors that dynamic complexity can introduce?
<--- Score

79. How can you manage cost down?
<--- Score

80. Are you aware of what could cause a problem?
<--- Score

81. How will measures be used to manage and adapt?
<--- Score

82. Where is it measured?
<--- Score

83. Are there measurements based on task performance?
<--- Score

84. How do you verify and validate the hybrid clouds data?
<--- Score

85. What disadvantage does this cause for the user?
<--- Score

86. How will effects be measured?
<--- Score

87. Have you made assumptions about the shape of the future, particularly its impact on your customers

and competitors?
<--- Score

88. What tests verify requirements?
<--- Score

89. Among the hybrid clouds product and service cost to be estimated, which is considered hardest to estimate?
<--- Score

90. What users will be impacted?
<--- Score

91. At what cost?
<--- Score

92. Why do the measurements/indicators matter?
<--- Score

93. How do you verify the authenticity of the data and information used?
<--- Score

94. Does a hybrid clouds quantification method exist?
<--- Score

95. What harm might be caused?
<--- Score

96. How do your measurements capture actionable hybrid clouds information for use in exceeding your customers expectations and securing your customers engagement?
<--- Score

97. How can you reduce the costs of obtaining inputs?
<--- Score

98. How is the value delivered by hybrid clouds being measured?
<--- Score

99. Do you effectively measure and reward individual and team performance?
<--- Score

100. What measurements are being captured?
<--- Score

101. Are the hybrid clouds benefits worth its costs?
<--- Score

102. How do you measure efficient delivery of hybrid clouds services?
<--- Score

103. What is your hybrid clouds quality cost segregation study?
<--- Score

104. What is the root cause(s) of the problem?
<--- Score

105. Has a cost center been established?
<--- Score

106. Are supply costs steady or fluctuating?
<--- Score

107. Is it possible to estimate the impact of unanticipated complexity such as wrong or failed

assumptions, feedback, etcetera on proposed reforms?
<--- Score

108. How is performance measured?
<--- Score

109. How do you verify and develop ideas and innovations?
<--- Score

110. What does a Test Case verify?
<--- Score

111. What are the hybrid clouds investment costs?
<--- Score

112. What relevant entities could be measured?
<--- Score

113. Where can you go to verify the info?
<--- Score

114. Did you tackle the cause or the symptom?
<--- Score

115. Are actual costs in line with budgeted costs?
<--- Score

116. How are you verifying it?
<--- Score

117. What measurements are possible, practicable and meaningful?
<--- Score

118. Are the units of measure consistent?
<--- Score

119. What are the uncertainties surrounding estimates of impact?
<--- Score

120. Are there competing hybrid clouds priorities?
<--- Score

121. What are your operating costs?
<--- Score

122. What causes mismanagement?
<--- Score

123. How are costs allocated?
<--- Score

124. Are you taking your company in the direction of better and revenue or cheaper and cost?
<--- Score

125. Are there any easy-to-implement alternatives to hybrid clouds? Sometimes other solutions are available that do not require the cost implications of a full-blown project?
<--- Score

126. Why do you expend time and effort to implement measurement, for whom?
<--- Score

127. Are the measurements objective?
<--- Score

128. What are you verifying?
<--- Score

129. How do you verify your resources?
<--- Score

130. How do you verify performance?
<--- Score

131. How will costs be allocated?
<--- Score

132. Will hybrid clouds have an impact on current business continuity, disaster recovery processes and/ or infrastructure?
<--- Score

133. Do you verify that corrective actions were taken?
<--- Score

134. What would it cost to replace your technology?
<--- Score

135. What causes investor action?
<--- Score

136. How do you control the overall costs of your work processes?
<--- Score

Add up total points for this section:
_ _ _ _ _ = Total points for this section

Divided by: _ _ _ _ _ _ (number of statements answered) = _ _ _ _ _ _
Average score for this section

Transfer your score to the hybrid clouds Index at the beginning of the Self-Assessment.

CRITERION #4: ANALYZE:

INTENT: Analyze causes, assumptions and hypotheses.

In my belief, the answer to this question is clearly defined:

5 Strongly Agree

4 Agree

3 Neutral

2 Disagree

1 Strongly Disagree

1. How will the hybrid clouds data be captured?
<--- Score

2. What qualifications and skills do you need?
<--- Score

3. Who is involved with workflow mapping?
<--- Score

4. What are the hybrid clouds design outputs?

<--- Score

5. How do you ensure that the hybrid clouds opportunity is realistic?
<--- Score

6. Who qualifies to gain access to data?
<--- Score

7. What qualifications do hybrid clouds leaders need?
<--- Score

8. How many input/output points does it require?
<--- Score

9. Were Pareto charts (or similar) used to portray the 'heavy hitters' (or key sources of variation)?
<--- Score

10. When should a process be art not science?
<--- Score

11. What are your hybrid clouds processes?
<--- Score

12. What output to create?
<--- Score

13. How is the data gathered?
<--- Score

14. What qualifies as competition?
<--- Score

15. What are the revised rough estimates of the financial savings/opportunity for hybrid clouds

improvements?
<--- Score

16. What does the data say about the performance of the stakeholder process?
<--- Score

17. What are the personnel training and qualifications required?
<--- Score

18. Think about the functions involved in your hybrid clouds project, what processes flow from these functions?
<--- Score

19. What were the crucial 'moments of truth' on the process map?
<--- Score

20. Do you understand your management processes today?
<--- Score

21. What are your best practices for minimizing hybrid clouds project risk, while demonstrating incremental value and quick wins throughout the hybrid clouds project lifecycle?
<--- Score

22. What hybrid clouds data should be managed?
<--- Score

23. Did any value-added analysis or 'lean thinking' take place to identify some of the gaps shown on the 'as is' process map?

<--- Score

24. Is the suppliers process defined and controlled?
<--- Score

25. What hybrid clouds data should be collected?
<--- Score

26. What kind of crime could a potential new hire
have committed that would not only not disqualify
him/her from being hired by your organization,
but would actually indicate that he/she might be a
particularly good fit?
<--- Score

27. What is the cost of poor quality as supported by
the team's analysis?
<--- Score

28. What hybrid clouds data do you gather or use
now?
<--- Score

29. What were the financial benefits resulting from
any 'ground fruit or low-hanging fruit' (quick fixes)?
<--- Score

30. What is the hybrid clouds Driver?
<--- Score

31. How will corresponding data be collected?
<--- Score

32. Is there an established change management
process?
<--- Score

33. What is the oversight process?
<--- Score

34. Has data output been validated?
<--- Score

35. Is the performance gap determined?
<--- Score

36. Have any additional benefits been identified that will result from closing all or most of the gaps?
<--- Score

37. Should you invest in industry-recognized qualifications?
<--- Score

38. What did the team gain from developing a sub-process map?
<--- Score

39. How are outputs preserved and protected?
<--- Score

40. Is the final output clearly identified?
<--- Score

41. Can you add value to the current hybrid clouds decision-making process (largely qualitative) by incorporating uncertainty modeling (more quantitative)?
<--- Score

42. How can risk management be tied procedurally to process elements?

<--- Score

43. How is the hybrid clouds Value Stream Mapping managed?
<--- Score

44. What is the complexity of the output produced?
<--- Score

45. Do your leaders quickly bounce back from setbacks?
<--- Score

46. Do your employees have the opportunity to do what they do best everyday?
<--- Score

47. Have the problem and goal statements been updated to reflect the additional knowledge gained from the analyze phase?
<--- Score

48. How was the detailed process map generated, verified, and validated?
<--- Score

49. What quality tools were used to get through the analyze phase?
<--- Score

50. Are all staff in core hybrid clouds subjects Highly Qualified?
<--- Score

51. Did any additional data need to be collected?
<--- Score

52. What is the output?
<--- Score

53. What are the processes for audit reporting and management?
<--- Score

54. How will the change process be managed?
<--- Score

55. What tools were used to narrow the list of possible causes?
<--- Score

56. Has an output goal been set?
<--- Score

57. Do you have the authority to produce the output?
<--- Score

58. What systems/processes must you excel at?
<--- Score

59. Do staff qualifications match your project?
<--- Score

60. How do you implement and manage your work processes to ensure that they meet design requirements?
<--- Score

61. How much data can be collected in the given timeframe?
<--- Score

62. Is there a strict change management process?
<--- Score

63. What hybrid clouds metrics are outputs of the process?
<--- Score

64. How does the organization define, manage, and improve its hybrid clouds processes?
<--- Score

65. Do you, as a leader, bounce back quickly from setbacks?
<--- Score

66. What information qualified as important?
<--- Score

67. Where can you get qualified talent today?
<--- Score

68. Record-keeping requirements flow from the records needed as inputs, outputs, controls and for transformation of a hybrid clouds process, are the records needed as inputs to the hybrid clouds process available?
<--- Score

69. What hybrid clouds data will be collected?
<--- Score

70. What data is gathered?
<--- Score

71. What types of data do your hybrid clouds indicators require?

<--- Score

72. What training and qualifications will you need?
<--- Score

73. How do you define collaboration and team output?
<--- Score

74. How is the way you as the leader think and process information affecting your organizational culture?
<--- Score

75. Who will gather what data?
<--- Score

76. What is your organizations process which leads to recognition of value generation?
<--- Score

77. Was a cause-and-effect diagram used to explore the different types of causes (or sources of variation)?
<--- Score

78. How has the hybrid clouds data been gathered?
<--- Score

79. What are the best opportunities for value improvement?
<--- Score

80. How is hybrid clouds data gathered?
<--- Score

81. Are you missing hybrid clouds opportunities?
<--- Score

82. What tools were used to generate the list of possible causes?
<--- Score

83. How difficult is it to qualify what hybrid clouds ROI is?
<--- Score

84. Which hybrid clouds data should be retained?
<--- Score

85. How do your work systems and key work processes relate to and capitalize on your core competencies?
<--- Score

86. What, related to, hybrid clouds processes does your organization outsource?
<--- Score

87. What are your key performance measures or indicators and in-process measures for the control and improvement of your hybrid clouds processes?
<--- Score

88. Who gets your output?
<--- Score

89. How do you promote understanding that opportunity for improvement is not criticism of the status quo, or the people who created the status quo?
<--- Score

90. How do you use hybrid clouds data and information to support organizational decision

making and innovation?

<--- Score

91. What qualifications are necessary?

<--- Score

92. What process improvements will be needed?

<--- Score

93. How is data used for program management and improvement?

<--- Score

94. What are the hybrid clouds business drivers?

<--- Score

95. What resources go in to get the desired output?

<--- Score

96. What successful thing are you doing today that may be blinding you to new growth opportunities?

<--- Score

97. Is the hybrid clouds process severely broken such that a re-design is necessary?

<--- Score

98. Were there any improvement opportunities identified from the process analysis?

<--- Score

99. Is the gap/opportunity displayed and communicated in financial terms?

<--- Score

100. Are gaps between current performance and the

goal performance identified?

<--- Score

101. Were any designed experiments used to generate additional insight into the data analysis?

<--- Score

102. Are hybrid clouds changes recognized early enough to be approved through the regular process?

<--- Score

103. What are your outputs?

<--- Score

104. How do you measure the operational performance of your key work systems and processes, including productivity, cycle time, and other appropriate measures of process effectiveness, efficiency, and innovation?

<--- Score

105. Who will facilitate the team and process?

<--- Score

106. What do you need to qualify?

<--- Score

107. How do you identify specific hybrid clouds investment opportunities and emerging trends?

<--- Score

108. What are your current levels and trends in key measures or indicators of hybrid clouds product and process performance that are important to and directly serve your customers? How do these results compare with the performance of your competitors

and other organizations with similar offerings?
<--- Score

109. What are your current levels and trends in key hybrid clouds measures or indicators of product and process performance that are important to and directly serve your customers?
<--- Score

110. Do several people in different organizational units assist with the hybrid clouds process?
<--- Score

111. What qualifications are needed?
<--- Score

112. What process should you select for improvement?
<--- Score

113. How will the data be checked for quality?
<--- Score

114. How often will data be collected for measures?
<--- Score

115. Do quality systems drive continuous improvement?
<--- Score

116. What are the necessary qualifications?
<--- Score

117. What other jobs or tasks affect the performance of the steps in the hybrid clouds process?
<--- Score

118. What is the Value Stream Mapping?
<--- Score

119. A compounding model resolution with available relevant data can often provide insight towards a solution methodology; which hybrid clouds models, tools and techniques are necessary?
<--- Score

120. What internal processes need improvement?
<--- Score

121. Do your contracts/agreements contain data security obligations?
<--- Score

122. What data do you need to collect?
<--- Score

123. Have you defined which data is gathered how?
<--- Score

124. Is the required hybrid clouds data gathered?
<--- Score

125. Is there any way to speed up the process?
<--- Score

126. What are evaluation criteria for the output?
<--- Score

127. What other organizational variables, such as reward systems or communication systems, affect the performance of this hybrid clouds process?
<--- Score

128. What is your organizations system for selecting qualified vendors?
<--- Score

129. Who owns what data?
<--- Score

130. Identify an operational issue in your organization, for example, could a particular task be done more quickly or more efficiently by hybrid clouds?
<--- Score

131. Are all team members qualified for all tasks?
<--- Score

132. What will drive hybrid clouds change?
<--- Score

133. An organizationally feasible system request is one that considers the mission, goals and objectives of the organization, key questions are: is the hybrid clouds solution request practical and will it solve a problem or take advantage of an opportunity to achieve company goals?
<--- Score

134. What conclusions were drawn from the team's data collection and analysis? How did the team reach these conclusions?
<--- Score

135. Is pre-qualification of suppliers carried out?
<--- Score

136. How do mission and objectives affect the hybrid

clouds processes of your organization?
<--- Score

137. Is data and process analysis, root cause analysis and quantifying the gap/opportunity in place?
<--- Score

138. Was a detailed process map created to amplify critical steps of the 'as is' stakeholder process?
<--- Score

139. Think about some of the processes you undertake within your organization, which do you own?
<--- Score

Add up total points for this section:
_ _ _ _ _ = Total points for this section

Divided by: _ _ _ _ _ _ (number of statements answered) = _ _ _ _ _ _
Average score for this section

Transfer your score to the hybrid clouds Index at the beginning of the Self-Assessment.

CRITERION #5: IMPROVE:

INTENT: Develop a practical solution.
Innovate, establish and test the
solution and to measure the results.

In my belief, the answer to this
question is clearly defined:

5 Strongly Agree

4 Agree

3 Neutral

2 Disagree

1 Strongly Disagree

1. How do you measure progress and evaluate
training effectiveness?
<--- Score

2. Is there a small-scale pilot for proposed
improvement(s)? What conclusions were drawn from
the outcomes of a pilot?
<--- Score

3. Who manages supplier risk management in your organization?
<--- Score

4. What is hybrid clouds risk?
<--- Score

5. Is there a cost/benefit analysis of optimal solution(s)?
<--- Score

6. When you map the key players in your own work and the types/domains of relationships with them, which relationships do you find easy and which challenging, and why?
<--- Score

7. How do you go about comparing hybrid clouds approaches/solutions?
<--- Score

8. Is the hybrid clouds documentation thorough?
<--- Score

9. Are the risks fully understood, reasonable and manageable?
<--- Score

10. Do you have the optimal project management team structure?
<--- Score

11. Which of the recognised risks out of all risks can be most likely transferred?
<--- Score

12. How can the phases of hybrid clouds development be identified?
<--- Score

13. Who will be responsible for documenting the hybrid clouds requirements in detail?
<--- Score

14. How can skill-level changes improve hybrid clouds?
<--- Score

15. For decision problems, how do you develop a decision statement?
<--- Score

16. What strategies for hybrid clouds improvement are successful?
<--- Score

17. What are the hybrid clouds security risks?
<--- Score

18. What tools were used to tap into the creativity and encourage 'outside the box' thinking?
<--- Score

19. Explorations of the frontiers of hybrid clouds will help you build influence, improve hybrid clouds, optimize decision making, and sustain change, what is your approach?
<--- Score

20. How do you mitigate hybrid clouds risk?
<--- Score

21. How do you improve productivity?
<--- Score

22. What can you do to improve?
<--- Score

23. Are procedures documented for managing hybrid clouds risks?
<--- Score

24. Are confused. so what are the most misunderstood facts about hybrid clouds among all stakeholders?
<--- Score

25. Is any hybrid clouds documentation required?
<--- Score

26. What is the team's contingency plan for potential problems occurring in implementation?
<--- Score

27. Risk Identification: What are the possible risk events your organization faces in relation to hybrid clouds?
<--- Score

28. What risks do you need to manage?
<--- Score

29. What error proofing will be done to address some of the discrepancies observed in the 'as is' process?
<--- Score

30. What is the implementation plan?
<--- Score

31. Does a good decision guarantee a good outcome?
<--- Score

32. Why improve in the first place?
<--- Score

33. How can you better manage risk?
<--- Score

34. How do you decide how much to remunerate an employee?
<--- Score

35. How can you improve hybrid clouds?
<--- Score

36. What to do with the results or outcomes of measurements?
<--- Score

37. Is the scope clearly documented?
<--- Score

38. What are the concrete hybrid clouds results?
<--- Score

39. How do you manage and improve your hybrid clouds work systems to deliver customer value and achieve organizational success and sustainability?
<--- Score

40. How significant is the improvement in the eyes of the end user?
<--- Score

41. How do you improve hybrid clouds service perception, and satisfaction?
<--- Score

42. What are the implications of the one critical hybrid clouds decision 10 minutes, 10 months, and 10 years from now?
<--- Score

43. Can you identify any significant risks or exposures to hybrid clouds third- parties (vendors, service providers, alliance partners etc) that concern you?
<--- Score

44. Risk factors: what are the characteristics of hybrid clouds that make it risky?
<--- Score

45. What needs improvement? Why?
<--- Score

46. Can the solution be designed and implemented within an acceptable time period?
<--- Score

47. Who should make the hybrid clouds decisions?
<--- Score

48. What attendant changes will need to be made to ensure that the solution is successful?
<--- Score

49. How will you know that you have improved?
<--- Score

50. For estimation problems, how do you develop an

estimation statement?

<--- Score

51. How are hybrid clouds risks managed?

<--- Score

52. What practices helps your organization to develop its capacity to recognize patterns?

<--- Score

53. Are risk management tasks balanced centrally and locally?

<--- Score

54. Who are the hybrid clouds decision-makers?

<--- Score

55. How is knowledge sharing about risk management improved?

<--- Score

56. Is the hybrid clouds solution sustainable?

<--- Score

57. How does your organization evaluate strategic hybrid clouds success?

<--- Score

58. What are your current levels and trends in key measures or indicators of workforce and leader development?

<--- Score

59. What alternative responses are available to manage risk?

<--- Score

60. Is hybrid clouds documentation maintained?
<--- Score

61. How do you deal with hybrid clouds risk?
<--- Score

62. Who makes the hybrid clouds decisions in your organization?
<--- Score

63. Are you assessing hybrid clouds and risk?
<--- Score

64. What current systems have to be understood and/or changed?
<--- Score

65. Are decisions made in a timely manner?
<--- Score

66. How will you recognize and celebrate results?
<--- Score

67. What tools do you use once you have decided on a hybrid clouds strategy and more importantly how do you choose?
<--- Score

68. What is hybrid clouds's impact on utilizing the best solution(s)?
<--- Score

69. How does the team improve its work?
<--- Score

70. What communications are necessary to support the implementation of the solution?
<--- Score

71. Can you integrate quality management and risk management?
<--- Score

72. What is the hybrid clouds's sustainability risk?
<--- Score

73. How is continuous improvement applied to risk management?
<--- Score

74. Are the key business and technology risks being managed?
<--- Score

75. In the past few months, what is the smallest change you have made that has had the biggest positive result? What was it about that small change that produced the large return?
<--- Score

76. What criteria will you use to assess your hybrid clouds risks?
<--- Score

77. Do the viable solutions scale to future needs?
<--- Score

78. Was a hybrid clouds charter developed?
<--- Score

79. What tools were most useful during the improve

phase?
<--- Score

80. Is there any other hybrid clouds solution?
<--- Score

81. Were any criteria developed to assist the team in testing and evaluating potential solutions?
<--- Score

82. Is the measure of success for hybrid clouds understandable to a variety of people?
<--- Score

83. How can you improve performance?
<--- Score

84. What hybrid clouds improvements can be made?
<--- Score

85. How do you measure risk?
<--- Score

86. Do you need to do a usability evaluation?
<--- Score

87. Do those selected for the hybrid clouds team have a good general understanding of what hybrid clouds is all about?
<--- Score

88. Who are the key stakeholders for the hybrid clouds evaluation?
<--- Score

89. How do you keep improving hybrid clouds?

<--- Score

90. Where do you need hybrid clouds improvement?
<--- Score

91. Who will be responsible for making the decisions to include or exclude requested changes once hybrid clouds is underway?
<--- Score

92. How do you link measurement and risk?
<--- Score

93. How scalable is your hybrid clouds solution?
<--- Score

94. Are the most efficient solutions problem-specific?
<--- Score

95. Have you identified breakpoints and/or risk tolerances that will trigger broad consideration of a potential need for intervention or modification of strategy?
<--- Score

96. What does the 'should be' process map/design look like?
<--- Score

97. Was a pilot designed for the proposed solution(s)?
<--- Score

98. What area needs the greatest improvement?
<--- Score

99. How do you define the solutions' scope?

<--- Score

100. How do you measure improved hybrid clouds service perception, and satisfaction?
<--- Score

101. What do you want to improve?
<--- Score

102. Who are the hybrid clouds decision makers?
<--- Score

103. What resources are required for the improvement efforts?
<--- Score

104. Who controls key decisions that will be made?
<--- Score

105. Are risk triggers captured?
<--- Score

106. Have you achieved hybrid clouds improvements?
<--- Score

107. Do you cover the five essential competencies: Communication, Collaboration,Innovation, Adaptability, and Leadership that improve an organizations ability to leverage the new hybrid clouds in a volatile global economy?
<--- Score

108. What lessons, if any, from a pilot were incorporated into the design of the full-scale solution?
<--- Score

109. What is the risk?
<--- Score

110. How risky is your organization?
<--- Score

111. At what point will vulnerability assessments
be performed once hybrid clouds is put into
production (e.g., ongoing Risk Management after
implementation)?
<--- Score

112. How will you know that a change is an
improvement?
<--- Score

113. hybrid clouds risk decisions: whose call Is It?
<--- Score

114. What were the underlying assumptions on the
cost-benefit analysis?
<--- Score

115. Is risk periodically assessed?
<--- Score

116. Who do you report hybrid clouds results to?
<--- Score

117. What should a proof of concept or pilot
accomplish?
<--- Score

118. What are the expected hybrid clouds results?
<--- Score

119. To what extent does management recognize hybrid clouds as a tool to increase the results?
<--- Score

120. Is there a high likelihood that any recommendations will achieve their intended results?
<--- Score

121. Who manages hybrid clouds risk?
<--- Score

122. Would you develop a hybrid clouds Communication Strategy?
<--- Score

123. Who will be using the results of the measurement activities?
<--- Score

124. Do you combine technical expertise with business knowledge and hybrid clouds Key topics include lifecycles, development approaches, requirements and how to make a business case?
<--- Score

125. What were the criteria for evaluating a hybrid clouds pilot?
<--- Score

126. Is supporting hybrid clouds documentation required?
<--- Score

127. What assumptions are made about the solution and approach?
<--- Score

128. What tools were used to evaluate the potential solutions?
<--- Score

129. Who controls the risk?
<--- Score

130. How are policy decisions made and where?
<--- Score

131. Do vendor agreements bring new compliance risk ?
<--- Score

132. Will the controls trigger any other risks?
<--- Score

133. How do you manage hybrid clouds risk?
<--- Score

134. If you could go back in time five years, what decision would you make differently? What is your best guess as to what decision you're making today you might regret five years from now?
<--- Score

135. Which hybrid clouds solution is appropriate?
<--- Score

136. Is the hybrid clouds risk managed?
<--- Score

137. What is the magnitude of the improvements?
<--- Score

138. Risk events: what are the things that could go wrong?
<--- Score

Add up total points for this section:
_____ = Total points for this section

Divided by: _____ (number of
statements answered) = _____
Average score for this section

Transfer your score to the hybrid clouds
Index at the beginning of the Self-
Assessment.

CRITERION #6: CONTROL:

INTENT: Implement the practical solution. Maintain the performance and correct possible complications.

In my belief, the answer to this question is clearly defined:

5 Strongly Agree

4 Agree

3 Neutral

2 Disagree

1 Strongly Disagree

1. Are new process steps, standards, and documentation ingrained into normal operations? <--- Score

2. In the case of a hybrid clouds project, the criteria for the audit derive from implementation objectives, an audit of a hybrid clouds project involves assessing whether the recommendations outlined for implementation have been met, can you track that

any hybrid clouds project is implemented as planned, and is it working?

<--- Score

3. Has the improved process and its steps been standardized?

<--- Score

4. How will you measure your QA plan's effectiveness?

<--- Score

5. Will your goals reflect your program budget?

<--- Score

6. Are the hybrid clouds standards challenging?

<--- Score

7. How widespread is its use?

<--- Score

8. How might the group capture best practices and lessons learned so as to leverage improvements?

<--- Score

9. Do you monitor the hybrid clouds decisions made and fine tune them as they evolve?

<--- Score

10. Is the hybrid clouds test/monitoring cost justified?

<--- Score

11. How do controls support value?

<--- Score

12. Who sets the hybrid clouds standards?

<--- Score

13. Implementation Planning: is a pilot needed to test the changes before a full roll out occurs?
<--- Score

14. How will the process owner and team be able to hold the gains?
<--- Score

15. What are the critical parameters to watch?
<--- Score

16. Will existing staff require re-training, for example, to learn new business processes?
<--- Score

17. How do senior leaders actions reflect a commitment to the organizations hybrid clouds values?
<--- Score

18. What are you attempting to measure/monitor?
<--- Score

19. How is hybrid clouds project cost planned, managed, monitored?
<--- Score

20. Is knowledge gained on process shared and institutionalized?
<--- Score

21. Who has control over resources?
<--- Score

22. How will report readings be checked to effectively

monitor performance?
<--- Score

23. Do the hybrid clouds decisions you make today help people and the planet tomorrow?
<--- Score

24. How do your controls stack up?
<--- Score

25. What is the standard for acceptable hybrid clouds performance?
<--- Score

26. Has the hybrid clouds value of standards been quantified?
<--- Score

27. How do you plan for the cost of succession?
<--- Score

28. Is a response plan in place for when the input, process, or output measures indicate an 'out-of-control' condition?
<--- Score

29. What are the key elements of your hybrid clouds performance improvement system, including your evaluation, organizational learning, and innovation processes?
<--- Score

30. Act/Adjust: What Do you Need to Do Differently?
<--- Score

31. Will the team be available to assist members in

planning investigations?

<--- Score

32. What is the best design framework for hybrid clouds organization now that, in a post industrial-age if the top-down, command and control model is no longer relevant?

<--- Score

33. Are suggested corrective/restorative actions indicated on the response plan for known causes to problems that might surface?

<--- Score

34. What is the recommended frequency of auditing?

<--- Score

35. Is there a documented and implemented monitoring plan?

<--- Score

36. How do you select, collect, align, and integrate hybrid clouds data and information for tracking daily operations and overall organizational performance, including progress relative to strategic objectives and action plans?

<--- Score

37. Is there a recommended audit plan for routine surveillance inspections of hybrid clouds's gains?

<--- Score

38. Can you adapt and adjust to changing hybrid clouds situations?

<--- Score

39. What hybrid clouds standards are applicable?
<--- Score

40. How can you best use all of your knowledge repositories to enhance learning and sharing?
<--- Score

41. Is there a transfer of ownership and knowledge to process owner and process team tasked with the responsibilities.
<--- Score

42. What are your results for key measures or indicators of the accomplishment of your hybrid clouds strategy and action plans, including building and strengthening core competencies?
<--- Score

43. Does the hybrid clouds performance meet the customer's requirements?
<--- Score

44. Who controls critical resources?
<--- Score

45. What is your theory of human motivation, and how does your compensation plan fit with that view?
<--- Score

46. How will the process owner verify improvement in present and future sigma levels, process capabilities?
<--- Score

47. Is reporting being used or needed?
<--- Score

48. How do you encourage people to take control and responsibility?
<--- Score

49. Does job training on the documented procedures need to be part of the process team's education and training?
<--- Score

50. Is there a standardized process?
<--- Score

51. Are controls in place and consistently applied?
<--- Score

52. Is a response plan established and deployed?
<--- Score

53. How will hybrid clouds decisions be made and monitored?
<--- Score

54. Are documented procedures clear and easy to follow for the operators?
<--- Score

55. What other areas of the group might benefit from the hybrid clouds team's improvements, knowledge, and learning?
<--- Score

56. Does the response plan contain a definite closed loop continual improvement scheme (e.g., plan-do-check-act)?
<--- Score

57. Where do ideas that reach policy makers and planners as proposals for hybrid clouds strengthening and reform actually originate?
<--- Score

58. Can support from partners be adjusted?
<--- Score

59. Are operating procedures consistent?
<--- Score

60. Are you measuring, monitoring and predicting hybrid clouds activities to optimize operations and profitability, and enhancing outcomes?
<--- Score

61. What key inputs and outputs are being measured on an ongoing basis?
<--- Score

62. Does a troubleshooting guide exist or is it needed?
<--- Score

63. Is new knowledge gained imbedded in the response plan?
<--- Score

64. How will the day-to-day responsibilities for monitoring and continual improvement be transferred from the improvement team to the process owner?
<--- Score

65. How do you establish and deploy modified action plans if circumstances require a shift in plans and rapid execution of new plans?

<--- Score

66. Will any special training be provided for results interpretation?
<--- Score

67. What are the known security controls?
<--- Score

68. Do you monitor the effectiveness of your hybrid clouds activities?
<--- Score

69. Is there a control plan in place for sustaining improvements (short and long-term)?
<--- Score

70. What is the control/monitoring plan?
<--- Score

71. Have new or revised work instructions resulted?
<--- Score

72. Is there an action plan in case of emergencies?
<--- Score

73. What should the next improvement project be that is related to hybrid clouds?
<--- Score

74. Are the planned controls in place?
<--- Score

75. Is there documentation that will support the successful operation of the improvement?
<--- Score

76. How do you plan on providing proper recognition and disclosure of supporting companies?
<--- Score

77. Against what alternative is success being measured?
<--- Score

78. What is your plan to assess your security risks?
<--- Score

79. What quality tools were useful in the control phase?
<--- Score

80. Are the planned controls working?
<--- Score

81. What should you measure to verify efficiency gains?
<--- Score

82. Who is the hybrid clouds process owner?
<--- Score

83. Are pertinent alerts monitored, analyzed and distributed to appropriate personnel?
<--- Score

84. What adjustments to the strategies are needed?
<--- Score

85. How will input, process, and output variables be checked to detect for sub-optimal conditions?
<--- Score

86. Who will be in control?
<--- Score

87. Does hybrid clouds appropriately measure and monitor risk?
<--- Score

88. Is there a hybrid clouds Communication plan covering who needs to get what information when?
<--- Score

89. Backup needs are often overlooked with hybrid clouds. Do you plan to use your legacy system to back up cloud-based virtual machines?
<--- Score

90. How is change control managed?
<--- Score

91. What do your reports reflect?
<--- Score

92. What are customers monitoring?
<--- Score

93. How do you spread information?
<--- Score

94. What do you stand for--and what are you against?
<--- Score

95. What other systems, operations, processes, and infrastructures (hiring practices, staffing, training, incentives/rewards, metrics/dashboards/scorecards, etc.) need updates, additions, changes, or deletions

in order to facilitate knowledge transfer and improvements?

<--- Score

96. What do you measure to verify effectiveness gains?

<--- Score

97. How will new or emerging customer needs/ requirements be checked/communicated to orient the process toward meeting the new specifications and continually reducing variation?

<--- Score

98. How likely is the current hybrid clouds plan to come in on schedule or on budget?

<--- Score

99. How do you monitor usage and cost?

<--- Score

100. Are there documented procedures?

<--- Score

Add up total points for this section:
_____ = Total points for this section

Divided by: _____ (number of statements answered) = _____
Average score for this section

Transfer your score to the hybrid clouds Index at the beginning of the Self-Assessment.

CRITERION #7: SUSTAIN:

INTENT: Retain the benefits.

In my belief, the answer to this question is clearly defined:

5 Strongly Agree

4 Agree

3 Neutral

2 Disagree

1 Strongly Disagree

1. Would you rather sell to knowledgeable and informed customers or to uninformed customers?
<--- Score

2. What counts that you are not counting?
<--- Score

3. What is your hybrid clouds strategy?
<--- Score

4. How do you ensure that implementations of hybrid

clouds products are done in a way that ensures safety?

<--- Score

5. What are current hybrid clouds paradigms?

<--- Score

6. What is your BATNA (best alternative to a negotiated agreement)?

<--- Score

7. How do senior leaders deploy your organizations vision and values through your leadership system, to the workforce, to key suppliers and partners, and to customers and other stakeholders, as appropriate?

<--- Score

8. How do you keep records, of what?

<--- Score

9. Is your basic point _____ or _____?

<--- Score

10. Do you think hybrid clouds accomplishes the goals you expect it to accomplish?

<--- Score

11. How will you ensure you get what you expected?

<--- Score

12. What are the challenges?

<--- Score

13. What new services of functionality will be implemented next with hybrid clouds ?

<--- Score

14. What are strategies for increasing support and reducing opposition?
<--- Score

15. Are hybrid clouds the secret weapon of Asia Pacific enterprises?
<--- Score

16. What are your personal philosophies regarding hybrid clouds and how do they influence your work?
<--- Score

17. What could happen if you do not do it?
<--- Score

18. What is the funding source for this project?
<--- Score

19. If you were responsible for initiating and implementing major changes in your organization, what steps might you take to ensure acceptance of those changes?
<--- Score

20. Why will customers want to buy your organizations products/services?
<--- Score

21. How do you govern and fulfill your societal responsibilities?
<--- Score

22. How will you motivate the stakeholders with the least vested interest?
<--- Score

23. Where can you break convention?
<--- Score

24. Are you making progress, and are you making progress as hybrid clouds leaders?
<--- Score

25. What are the business benefits of hybrid clouds?
<--- Score

26. Who is responsible for ensuring appropriate resources (time, people and money) are allocated to hybrid clouds?
<--- Score

27. Think of your hybrid clouds project, what are the main functions?
<--- Score

28. If you find that you havent accomplished one of the goals for one of the steps of the hybrid clouds strategy, what will you do to fix it?
<--- Score

29. How do you accomplish your long range hybrid clouds goals?
<--- Score

30. What hybrid clouds modifications can you make work for you?
<--- Score

31. Is hybrid clouds realistic, or are you setting yourself up for failure?

<--- Score

32. Who do you want your customers to become?
<--- Score

33. What will be the consequences to the stakeholder (financial, reputation etc) if hybrid clouds does not go ahead or fails to deliver the objectives?
<--- Score

34. How do you create buy-in?
<--- Score

35. What happens if you do not have enough funding?
<--- Score

36. How do customers see your organization?
<--- Score

37. What is the estimated value of the project?
<--- Score

38. How do you engage the workforce, in addition to satisfying them?
<--- Score

39. Can you do all this work?
<--- Score

40. How do you provide a safe environment -physically and emotionally?
<--- Score

41. How important is hybrid clouds to the user organizations mission?

<--- Score

42. What is the source of the strategies for hybrid clouds strengthening and reform?
<--- Score

43. If you got fired and a new hire took your place, what would she do different?
<--- Score

44. Who are your customers?
<--- Score

45. What would have to be true for the option on the table to be the best possible choice?
<--- Score

46. If you weren't already in this business, would you enter it today? And if not, what are you going to do about it?
<--- Score

47. Who else should you help?
<--- Score

48. What knowledge, skills and characteristics mark a good hybrid clouds project manager?
<--- Score

49. What are you trying to prove to yourself, and how might it be hijacking your life and business success?
<--- Score

50. What have you done to protect your business from competitive encroachment?
<--- Score

51. What are the rules and assumptions your industry operates under? What if the opposite were true?
<--- Score

52. What is the overall business strategy?
<--- Score

53. Why should people listen to you?
<--- Score

54. Who is responsible for hybrid clouds?
<--- Score

55. What are the top 3 things at the forefront of your hybrid clouds agendas for the next 3 years?
<--- Score

56. Is there any existing hybrid clouds governance structure?
<--- Score

57. Do you think you know, or do you know you know ?
<--- Score

58. How long will it take to change?
<--- Score

59. How do you keep the momentum going?
<--- Score

60. Operational - will it work?
<--- Score

61. How are you doing compared to your industry?

<--- Score

62. At what moment would you think; Will I get fired?
<--- Score

63. What is it like to work for you?
<--- Score

64. Is your strategy driving your strategy? Or is the way in which you allocate resources driving your strategy?
<--- Score

65. What is something you believe that nearly no one agrees with you on?
<--- Score

66. Can the schedule be done in the given time?
<--- Score

67. Who is responsible for errors?
<--- Score

68. What may be the consequences for the performance of an organization if all stakeholders are not consulted regarding hybrid clouds?
<--- Score

69. What are your most important goals for the strategic hybrid clouds objectives?
<--- Score

70. What are specific hybrid clouds rules to follow?
<--- Score

71. What is the range of capabilities?

<--- Score

72. What goals did you miss?
<--- Score

73. Are you / should you be revolutionary or evolutionary?
<--- Score

74. Ask yourself: how would you do this work if you only had one staff member to do it?
<--- Score

75. Are all key stakeholders present at all Structured Walkthroughs?
<--- Score

76. Is there a work around that you can use?
<--- Score

77. Which functions and people interact with the supplier and or customer?
<--- Score

78. Political -is anyone trying to undermine this project?
<--- Score

79. How can you incorporate support to ensure safe and effective use of hybrid clouds into the services that you provide?
<--- Score

80. How will you insure seamless interoperability of hybrid clouds moving forward?
<--- Score

81. In the past year, what have you done (or could you have done) to increase the accurate perception of your company/brand as ethical and honest?
<--- Score

82. Are hybrid clouds in your future?
<--- Score

83. What is an unauthorized commitment?
<--- Score

84. Who have you, as a company, historically been when you've been at your best?
<--- Score

85. Which models, tools and techniques are necessary?
<--- Score

86. How will you know that the hybrid clouds project has been successful?
<--- Score

87. In retrospect, of the projects that you pulled the plug on, what percent do you wish had been allowed to keep going, and what percent do you wish had ended earlier?
<--- Score

88. How do you lead with hybrid clouds in mind?
<--- Score

89. What was the last experiment you ran?
<--- Score

90. What is your competitive advantage?
<--- Score

91. If you do not follow, then how to lead?
<--- Score

92. Why do and why don't your customers like your organization?
<--- Score

93. What should you stop doing?
<--- Score

94. What business benefits will hybrid clouds goals deliver if achieved?
<--- Score

95. Will there be any necessary staff changes (redundancies or new hires)?
<--- Score

96. Why is hybrid clouds important for you now?
<--- Score

97. What is your question? Why?
<--- Score

98. Why is it important to have senior management support for a hybrid clouds project?
<--- Score

99. What is your formula for success in hybrid clouds ?
<--- Score

100. Who do you think the world wants your organization to be?

<--- Score

101. Who will determine interim and final deadlines?
<--- Score

102. What did you miss in the interview for the worst hire you ever made?
<--- Score

103. Are the criteria for selecting recommendations stated?
<--- Score

104. Which hybrid clouds goals are the most important?
<--- Score

105. What role does communication play in the success or failure of a hybrid clouds project?
<--- Score

106. How do you make it meaningful in connecting hybrid clouds with what users do day-to-day?
<--- Score

107. Who will be responsible for deciding whether hybrid clouds goes ahead or not after the initial investigations?
<--- Score

108. What would you recommend your friend do if he/she were facing this dilemma?
<--- Score

109. What one word do you want to own in the minds of your customers, employees, and partners?

<--- Score

110. What unique value proposition (UVP) do you offer?
<--- Score

111. How do you transition from the baseline to the target?
<--- Score

112. In a project to restructure hybrid clouds outcomes, which stakeholders would you involve?
<--- Score

113. Who are the key stakeholders?
<--- Score

114. What are internal and external hybrid clouds relations?
<--- Score

115. Is hybrid clouds dependent on the successful delivery of a current project?
<--- Score

116. What happens when a new employee joins the organization?
<--- Score

117. Why are many companies considering public cloud in the first place and why does it differ from private and hybrid clouds?
<--- Score

118. How do you know if you are successful?
<--- Score

119. Is there any reason to believe the opposite of my current belief?
<--- Score

120. How do you deal with hybrid clouds changes?
<--- Score

121. Do you feel that more should be done in the hybrid clouds area?
<--- Score

122. Do you have the right capabilities and capacities?
<--- Score

123. What is the craziest thing you can do?
<--- Score

124. What is the purpose of hybrid clouds in relation to the mission?
<--- Score

125. What must you excel at?
<--- Score

126. Is maximizing hybrid clouds protection the same as minimizing hybrid clouds loss?
<--- Score

127. How do you manage hybrid clouds Knowledge Management (KM)?
<--- Score

128. Is the hybrid clouds organization completing tasks effectively and efficiently?
<--- Score

129. What is a feasible sequencing of reform initiatives over time?

<--- Score

130. Are assumptions made in hybrid clouds stated explicitly?

<--- Score

131. What happens at your organization when people fail?

<--- Score

132. What are the success criteria that will indicate that hybrid clouds objectives have been met and the benefits delivered?

<--- Score

133. Marketing budgets are tighter, consumers are more skeptical, and social media has changed forever the way we talk about hybrid clouds, how do you gain traction?

<--- Score

134. What hybrid clouds skills are most important?

<--- Score

135. Who will provide the final approval of hybrid clouds deliverables?

<--- Score

136. What projects are going on in the organization today, and what resources are those projects using from the resource pools?

<--- Score

137. What is the recommended frequency of auditing?
<--- Score

138. What information is critical to your organization that your executives are ignoring?
<--- Score

139. How do you go about securing hybrid clouds?
<--- Score

140. Who are four people whose careers you have enhanced?
<--- Score

141. What are the potential basics of hybrid clouds fraud?
<--- Score

142. Instead of going to current contacts for new ideas, what if you reconnected with dormant contacts--the people you used to know? If you were going reactivate a dormant tie, who would it be?
<--- Score

143. What are the key enablers to make this hybrid clouds move?
<--- Score

144. Whom among your colleagues do you trust, and for what?
<--- Score

145. Which individuals, teams or departments will be involved in hybrid clouds?
<--- Score

146. What you are going to do to affect the numbers?
<--- Score

147. What management system can you use to leverage the hybrid clouds experience, ideas, and concerns of the people closest to the work to be done?
<--- Score

148. What are the short and long-term hybrid clouds goals?
<--- Score

149. What are you challenging?
<--- Score

150. What stupid rule would you most like to kill?
<--- Score

151. What trouble can you get into?
<--- Score

152. Can you maintain your growth without detracting from the factors that have contributed to your success?
<--- Score

153. Who is on the team?
<--- Score

154. How do you proactively clarify deliverables and hybrid clouds quality expectations?
<--- Score

155. What have been your experiences in defining long range hybrid clouds goals?

<--- Score

156. Will it be accepted by users?
<--- Score

157. Do you have past hybrid clouds successes?
<--- Score

158. Is it economical; do you have the time and money?
<--- Score

159. Who, on the executive team or the board, has spoken to a customer recently?
<--- Score

160. How do you maintain hybrid clouds's Integrity?
<--- Score

161. Is a hybrid clouds team work effort in place?
<--- Score

162. What relationships among hybrid clouds trends do you perceive?
<--- Score

163. Why not do hybrid clouds?
<--- Score

164. If you had to rebuild your organization without any traditional competitive advantages (i.e., no killer technology, promising research, innovative product/ service delivery model, etcetera), how would your people have to approach their work and collaborate together in order to create the necessary conditions for success?

<--- Score

165. What is the kind of project structure that would be appropriate for your hybrid clouds project, should it be formal and complex, or can it be less formal and relatively simple?
<--- Score

166. Who is the main stakeholder, with ultimate responsibility for driving hybrid clouds forward?
<--- Score

167. What are the gaps in your knowledge and experience?
<--- Score

168. When information truly is ubiquitous, when reach and connectivity are completely global, when computing resources are infinite, and when a whole new set of impossibilities are not only possible, but happening, what will that do to your business?
<--- Score

169. How do you listen to customers to obtain actionable information?
<--- Score

170. How do you set hybrid clouds stretch targets and how do you get people to not only participate in setting these stretch targets but also that they strive to achieve these?
<--- Score

Add up total points for this section:
_ _ _ _ _ = Total points for this section

Divided by: _____ (number of
statements answered) = _____
Average score for this section

Transfer your score to the hybrid clouds
Index at the beginning of the Self-
Assessment.

Hybrid Clouds and Managing Projects, Criteria for Project Managers:

1.0 Initiating Process Group: Hybrid Clouds

1. How will you know you did it?

2. During which stage of Risk planning are modeling techniques used to determine overall effects of risks on Hybrid Clouds project objectives for high probability, high impact risks?

3. Based on your Hybrid Clouds project communication management plan, what worked well?

4. Are you properly tracking the progress of the Hybrid Clouds project and communicating the status to stakeholders?

5. Although the Hybrid Clouds project manager does not directly manage procurement and contracting activities, who does manage procurement and contracting activities in your organization then if not the PM?

6. Will the Hybrid Clouds project meet the client requirements, and will it achieve the business success criteria that justified doing the Hybrid Clouds project in the first place?

7. Were decisions made in a timely manner?

8. Professionals want to know what is expected from them what are the deliverables?

9. What were things that you did well, and could

improve, and how?

10. Mitigate. what will you do to minimize the impact should the risk event occur?

11. Are you certain deliverables are properly completed and meet quality standards?

12. Do you know the Hybrid Clouds projects goal, purpose and objectives?

13. How do you help others satisfy needs?

14. What will be the pressing issues of tomorrow?

15. For technology Hybrid Clouds projects only: Are all production support stakeholders (Business unit, technical support, & user) prepared for implementation with appropriate contingency plans?

16. Have the stakeholders identified all individual requirements pertaining to business process?

17. What are the inputs required to produce the deliverables?

18. The process to Manage Stakeholders is part of which process group?

19. Do you know all the stakeholders impacted by the Hybrid Clouds project and what needs are?

20. If action is called for, what form should it take?

1.1 Project Charter: Hybrid Clouds

21. What are the constraints?

22. Why Outsource?

23. What barriers do you predict to your success?

24. What is the justification?

25. What are the assigned resources?

26. Must Have?

27. What goes into your Hybrid Clouds project Charter?

28. What ideas do you have for initial tests of change (PDSA cycles)?

29. How are Hybrid Clouds projects different from operations?

30. What are the known stakeholder requirements?

31. Customer benefits: what customer requirements does this Hybrid Clouds project address?

32. What material?

33. Run it as as a startup?

34. What does it need to do?

35. How will you know a change is an improvement?

36. Why have you chosen the aim you have set forth?

37. Where and how does the team fit within your organization structure?

38. What metrics could you look at?

39. What is the purpose of the Hybrid Clouds project?

40. Who will take notes, document decisions?

1.2 Stakeholder Register: Hybrid Clouds

41. What & Why?

42. How much influence do they have on the Hybrid Clouds project?

43. What is the power of the stakeholder?

44. How will reports be created?

45. Who are the stakeholders?

46. How should employers make voices heard?

47. Is your organization ready for change?

48. Who is managing stakeholder engagement?

49. Who wants to talk about Security?

50. What opportunities exist to provide communications?

51. How big is the gap?

52. What are the major Hybrid Clouds project milestones requiring communications or providing communications opportunities?

1.3 Stakeholder Analysis Matrix: Hybrid Clouds

53. Who has the power to influence the outcomes of the work?

54. What do you Evaluate?

55. Will the impacts be local, national or international?

56. Would it be fair to say that cost is a controlling criteria?

57. Who will be affected by the Hybrid Clouds project?

58. What tools would help you communicate?

59. What can the Hybrid Clouds projects outcome be used for?

60. Where are the good opportunities facing your organizations development?

61. How do they affect the Hybrid Clouds project and its outcomes?

62. Who will be responsible for managing the outcome?

63. Why do you care?

64. Do any safeguard policies apply to the Hybrid Clouds project?

65. Processes and systems, etc?

66. What do people from other organizations see as your strengths?

67. What are innovative aspects of your organization?

68. Are you going to weigh the stakeholders?

69. Who holds positions of responsibility in interested organizations?

70. Are the required specifications for products or services changing?

71. Partnership opportunities/synergies?

72. Market demand?

2.0 Planning Process Group: Hybrid Clouds

73. To what extent have the target population and participants made the activities own, taking an active role in it?

74. Why do it Hybrid Clouds projects fail?

75. How can you make your needs known?

76. What is involved in Hybrid Clouds project scope management, and why is good Hybrid Clouds project scope management so important on information technology Hybrid Clouds projects?

77. To what extent are the visions and actions of the partners consistent or divergent with regard to the program?

78. Is the schedule for the set products being met?

79. On which process should team members spend the most time?

80. To what extent is the program helping to influence your organizations policy framework?

81. Mitigate. what will you do to minimize the impact should a risk event occur?

82. When developing the estimates for Hybrid Clouds project phases, you choose to add the individual

estimates for the activities that comprise each phase. What type of estimation method are you using?

83. If a task is partitionable, is this a sufficient condition to reduce the Hybrid Clouds project duration?

84. When will the Hybrid Clouds project be done?

85. How are the principles of aid effectiveness (ownership, alignment, management for development results and mutual responsibility) being applied in the Hybrid Clouds project?

86. Are there efficient coordination mechanisms to avoid overloading the counterparts, participating stakeholders?

87. How does activity resource estimation affect activity duration estimation?

88. Is the Hybrid Clouds project making progress in helping to achieve the set results?

89. How many days can task X be late in starting without affecting the Hybrid Clouds project completion date?

90. What input will you be required to provide the Hybrid Clouds project team?

91. In what way has the program contributed towards the issue culture and development included on the public agenda?

2.1 Project Management Plan: Hybrid Clouds

92. Do the proposed changes from the Hybrid Clouds project include any significant risks to safety?

93. What is the business need?

94. Why Change?

95. Are the existing and future without-plan conditions reasonable and appropriate?

96. What worked well?

97. How do you manage integration?

98. Are calculations and results of analyzes essentially correct?

99. Was the peer (technical) review of the cost estimates duly coordinated with the cost estimate center of expertise and addressed in the review documentation and certification?

100. Does the implementation plan have an appropriate division of responsibilities?

101. Did the planning effort collaborate to develop solutions that integrate expertise, policies, programs, and Hybrid Clouds projects across entities?

102. How well are you able to manage your risk?

103. Who is the Hybrid Clouds project Manager?

104. Are there any Client staffing expectations?

105. If the Hybrid Clouds project management plan is a comprehensive document that guides you in Hybrid Clouds project execution and control, then what should it NOT contain?

106. Are there any windfall benefits that would accrue to the Hybrid Clouds project sponsor or other parties?

2.2 Scope Management Plan: Hybrid Clouds

107. Is each item clearly and completely defined?

108. How do you handle uncertainty or conflict?

109. Are procurement deliverables arriving on time and to specification?

110. Describe how the deliverables will be verified against the Hybrid Clouds project scope. To whom will the deliverables be first presented for inspection and verification?

111. Pop quiz – which are the same inputs as in scope planning?

112. Have reserves been created to address risks?

113. Has a structured approach been used to break work effort into manageable components (WBS)?

114. Where do scope management processes fit in?

115. Does the Hybrid Clouds project team have the skills necessary to successfully complete current Hybrid Clouds project(s) and support the application?

116. Why is a scope management plan important?

117. Are the schedule estimates reasonable given the Hybrid Clouds project?

118. Has the business need been clearly defined?

119. Have activity relationships and interdependencies within tasks been adequately identified?

120. Are you doing what you have set out to do?

121. Materials available for performing the work?

122. Has appropriate allowance been made for the effect of the learning curve on all personnel joining the Hybrid Clouds project who do not have the required prior industry, functional & technical expertise?

123. Have the scope, objectives, costs, benefits and impacts been communicated to all involved and/or impacted stakeholders and work groups?

124. Is your organization structure for both tracking & controlling the budget well defined and assigned to a specific individual?

125. Was the scope definition used in task sequencing?

126. Did your Hybrid Clouds project ask for this?

2.3 Requirements Management Plan: Hybrid Clouds

127. How will you communicate scheduled tasks to other team members?

128. Could inaccurate or incomplete requirements in this Hybrid Clouds project create a serious risk for the business?

129. How often will the reporting occur?

130. Have stakeholders been instructed in the Change Control process?

131. Do you really need to write this document at all?

132. After the requirements are gathered and set forth on the requirements register, theyre little more than a laundry list of items. Some may be duplicates, some might conflict with others and some will be too broad or too vague to understand. Describe how the requirements will be analyzed. Who will perform the analysis?

133. The wbs is developed as part of a joint planning session. and how do you know that youhave done this right?

134. What is a problem?

135. Business analysis scope?

136. What are you trying to do?

137. Do you know which stakeholders will participate in the requirements effort?

138. Will you use an assessment of the Hybrid Clouds project environment as a tool to discover risk to the requirements process?

139. Who will do the reporting and to whom will reports be delivered?

140. Who has the authority to reject Hybrid Clouds project requirements?

141. If it exists, where is it housed?

142. Will the product release be stable and mature enough to be deployed in the user community?

143. How will requirements be managed?

144. How do you know that you have done this right?

145. Did you distinguish the scope of work the contractor(s) will be required to do?

146. Will you have access to stakeholders when you need them?

2.4 Requirements Documentation: Hybrid Clouds

147. How does the proposed Hybrid Clouds project contribute to the overall objectives of your organization?

148. Are there any requirements conflicts?

149. Where do you define what is a customer, what are the attributes of customer?

150. Can the requirement be changed without a large impact on other requirements?

151. What is effective documentation?

152. Do technical resources exist?

153. How to document system requirements?

154. Where do system and software requirements come from, what are sources?

155. What images does it conjure?

156. What is the risk associated with the technology?

157. What marketing channels do you want to use: e-mail, letter or sms?

158. Where are business rules being captured?

159. Does your organization restrict technical alternatives?

160. How do you get the user to tell you what they want?

161. Who is involved?

162. What are the potential disadvantages/ advantages?

163. Are all functions required by the customer included?

164. Does the system provide the functions which best support the customers needs?

165. What can tools do for us?

166. Is new technology needed?

2.5 Requirements Traceability Matrix: Hybrid Clouds

167. Will you use a Requirements Traceability Matrix?

168. Describe the process for approving requirements so they can be added to the traceability matrix and Hybrid Clouds project work can be performed. Will the Hybrid Clouds project requirements become approved in writing?

169. How small is small enough?

170. Why do you manage scope?

171. Why use a WBS?

172. Do you have a clear understanding of all subcontracts in place?

173. Is there a requirements traceability process in place?

174. How do you manage scope?

175. What is the WBS?

176. How will it affect the stakeholders personally in career?

177. What are the chronologies, contingencies, consequences, criteria?

178. What percentage of Hybrid Clouds projects are producing traceability matrices between requirements and other work products?

2.6 Project Scope Statement: Hybrid Clouds

179. Does the scope statement still need some clarity?

180. Is there an information system for the Hybrid Clouds project?

181. Elements that deal with providing the detail?

182. Risks?

183. Were potential customers involved early in the planning process?

184. Any new risks introduced or old risks impacted. Are there issues that could affect the existing requirements for the result, service, or product if the scope changes?

185. Are there specific processes you will use to evaluate and approve/reject changes?

186. Will you need a statement of work?

187. Will all Hybrid Clouds project issues be unconditionally tracked through the issue resolution process?

188. What went wrong?

189. Have the reports to be produced, distributed, and filed been defined?

190. How often will scope changes be reviewed?

191. Will the risk status be reported to management on a regular and frequent basis?

192. Is there a Quality Assurance Plan documented and filed?

193. Is an issue management process documented and filed?

194. What actions will be taken to mitigate the risk?

195. Did your Hybrid Clouds project ask for this?

196. Change management vs. change leadership - what is the difference?

197. Is the Hybrid Clouds project manager qualified and experienced in Hybrid Clouds project management?

198. Have you been able to thoroughly document the Hybrid Clouds projects assumptions and constraints?

2.7 Assumption and Constraint Log: Hybrid Clouds

199. Does the plan conform to standards?

200. What weaknesses do you have?

201. Is staff trained on the software technologies that are being used on the Hybrid Clouds project?

202. What does an audit system look like?

203. Do the requirements meet the standards of correctness, completeness, consistency, accuracy, and readability?

204. What strengths do you have?

205. Are there processes in place to ensure internal consistency between the source code components?

206. Diagrams and tables are included to account for complex concepts and increase overall readability?

207. Does the traceability documentation describe the tool and/or mechanism to be used to capture traceability throughout the life cycle?

208. Does the system design reflect the requirements?

209. Are best practices and metrics employed to identify issues, progress, performance, etc.?

210. How can you prevent/fix violations?

211. Do documented requirements exist for all critical components and areas, including technical, business, interfaces, performance, security and conversion requirements?

212. What to do at recovery?

213. Are you meeting your customers expectations consistently?

214. Contradictory information between document sections?

215. Model-building: what data-analytic strategies are useful when building proportional-hazards models?

216. How are new requirements or changes to requirements identified?

2.8 Work Breakdown Structure: Hybrid Clouds

217. Is the work breakdown structure (wbs) defined and is the scope of the Hybrid Clouds project clear with assigned deliverable owners?

218. When do you stop?

219. Who has to do it?

220. Why would you develop a Work Breakdown Structure?

221. Can you make it?

222. How many levels?

223. Is it a change in scope?

224. Where does it take place?

225. Do you need another level?

226. Is it still viable?

227. How much detail?

228. Why is it useful?

229. How far down?

230. When does it have to be done?

231. When would you develop a Work Breakdown Structure?

232. What is the probability that the Hybrid Clouds project duration will exceed xx weeks?

233. How big is a work-package?

2.9 WBS Dictionary: Hybrid Clouds

234. Budgets assigned to major functional organizations?

235. Is work properly classified as measured effort, LOE, or apportioned effort and appropriately separated?

236. Does the contractors system include procedures for measuring the performance of critical subcontractors?

237. Incurrence of actual indirect costs in excess of budgets, by element of expense?

238. Are budgets or values assigned to work packages and planning packages in terms of dollars, hours, or other measurable units?

239. Does the contractors system provide unit or lot costs when applicable?

240. What is the goal?

241. What is wrong with this Hybrid Clouds project?

242. Detailed schedules which support control account and work package start and completion dates/events?

243. Do procedures specify under what circumstances replanning of open work packages may occur, and the methods to be followed?

244. Are internal budgets for authorized, and not priced changes based on the contractors resource plan for accomplishing the work?

245. Are the rates for allocating costs from each indirect cost pool to contracts updated as necessary to ensure a realistic monthly allocation of indirect costs without significant year-end adjustments?

246. Knowledgeable Hybrid Clouds projections of future performance?

247. Does the contractor use objective results, design reviews and tests to trace schedule performance?

248. Are data elements (BCWS, BCWP, and ACWP) progressively summarized from the detail level to the contract level through the CWBS?

249. What should you drop in order to add something new?

250. Does the contractors system provide for determination of price variance by comparing planned Vs actual commitments?

251. Are indirect costs accumulated for comparison with the corresponding budgets?

252. Are the wbs and organizational levels for application of the Hybrid Clouds projected overhead costs identified?

253. Does the contractors system identify work accomplishment against the schedule plan?

2.10 Schedule Management Plan: Hybrid Clouds

254. Are action items captured and managed?

255. Are Hybrid Clouds project contact logs kept up to date?

256. Has your organization readiness assessment been conducted?

257. Does the schedule have reasonable float?

258. Are staff skills known and available for each task?

259. Are written status reports provided on a designated frequent basis?

260. Are assumptions being identified, recorded, analyzed, qualified and closed?

261. Is a payment system in place with proper reviews and approvals?

262. Is the communication plan being followed?

263. Has the budget been baselined?

264. Is a process for scheduling and reporting defined, including forms and formats?

265. Who is responsible for estimating the activity resources?

266. Are vendor invoices audited for accuracy before payment?

267. Have the key functions and capabilities been defined and assigned to each release or iteration?

268. What tools and techniques will be used to estimate activity resources?

269. Are updated Hybrid Clouds project time & resource estimates reasonable based on the current Hybrid Clouds project stage?

270. Is there a formal set of procedures supporting Issues Management?

271. Does the Hybrid Clouds project have quality set of schedule BOEs?

272. Does the Hybrid Clouds project have a formal Hybrid Clouds project Charter?

273. Does the Hybrid Clouds project have a Quality Culture?

2.11 Activity List: Hybrid Clouds

274. What did not go as well?

275. In what sequence?

276. How do you determine the late start (LS) for each activity?

277. What are the critical bottleneck activities?

278. What will be performed?

279. What is the probability the Hybrid Clouds project can be completed in xx weeks?

280. Are the required resources available or need to be acquired?

281. Where will it be performed?

282. When do the individual activities need to start and finish?

283. How can the Hybrid Clouds project be displayed graphically to better visualize the activities?

284. How difficult will it be to do specific activities on this Hybrid Clouds project?

285. What are you counting on?

286. Can you determine the activity that must finish, before this activity can start?

287. When will the work be performed?

288. What is your organizations history in doing similar activities?

289. What is the total time required to complete the Hybrid Clouds project if no delays occur?

290. How detailed should a Hybrid Clouds project get?

291. Is there anything planned that does not need to be here?

292. For other activities, how much delay can be tolerated?

2.12 Activity Attributes: Hybrid Clouds

293. What is the general pattern here?

294. Were there other ways you could have organized the data to achieve similar results?

295. How much activity detail is required?

296. What is missing?

297. Why?

298. Does your organization of the data change its meaning?

299. How else could the items be grouped?

300. Have you identified the Activity Leveling Priority code value on each activity?

301. Is there a trend during the year?

302. How difficult will it be to complete specific activities on this Hybrid Clouds project?

303. How do you manage time?

304. Resources to accomplish the work?

305. Time for overtime?

306. Have constraints been applied to the start and finish milestones for the phases?

307. Resource is assigned to?

308. Activity: what is Missing?

309. What conclusions/generalizations can you draw from this?

2.13 Milestone List: Hybrid Clouds

310. Information and research?

311. What specific improvements did you make to the Hybrid Clouds project proposal since the previous time?

312. Sustaining internal capabilities?

313. Which path is the critical path?

314. How late can the activity finish?

315. How will the milestone be verified?

316. What are your competitors vulnerabilities?

317. Reliability of data, plan predictability?

318. Identify critical paths (one or more) and which activities are on the critical path?

319. How soon can the activity finish?

320. Who will manage the Hybrid Clouds project on a day-to-day basis?

321. Calculate how long can activity be delayed?

322. Marketing - reach, distribution, awareness?

323. Competitive advantages?

324. Gaps in capabilities?

325. Describe your organizations strengths and core competencies. What factors will make your organization succeed?

326. Usps (unique selling points)?

327. Milestone pages should display the UserID of the person who added the milestone. Does a report or query exist that provides this audit information?

328. Can you derive how soon can the whole Hybrid Clouds project finish?

2.14 Network Diagram: Hybrid Clouds

329. Why must you schedule milestones, such as reviews, throughout the Hybrid Clouds project?

330. What job or jobs follow it?

331. What activities must occur simultaneously with this activity?

332. Where do you schedule uncertainty time?

333. What are the tools?

334. If the Hybrid Clouds project network diagram cannot change and you have extra personnel resources, what is the BEST thing to do?

335. What to do and When?

336. Exercise: what is the probability that the Hybrid Clouds project duration will exceed xx weeks?

337. What controls the start and finish of a job?

338. Are you on time?

339. Which type of network diagram allows you to depict four types of dependencies?

340. What job or jobs could run concurrently?

341. What can be done concurrently?

342. Planning: who, how long, what to do?

343. Review the logical flow of the network diagram. Take a look at which activities you have first and then sequence the activities. Do they make sense?

344. What is the probability of completing the Hybrid Clouds project in less that xx days?

345. Will crashing x weeks return more in benefits than it costs?

346. What is the lowest cost to complete this Hybrid Clouds project in xx weeks?

347. How difficult will it be to do specific activities on this Hybrid Clouds project?

348. Can you calculate the confidence level?

2.15 Activity Resource Requirements: Hybrid Clouds

349. Organizational Applicability?

350. What is the Work Plan Standard?

351. When does monitoring begin?

352. What are constraints that you might find during the Human Resource Planning process?

353. How many signatures do you require on a check and does this match what is in your policy and procedures?

354. Do you use tools like decomposition and rolling-wave planning to produce the activity list and other outputs?

355. How do you handle petty cash?

356. Are there unresolved issues that need to be addressed?

357. Which logical relationship does the PDM use most often?

358. Anything else?

359. Other support in specific areas?

360. Why do you do that?

2.16 Resource Breakdown Structure: Hybrid Clouds

361. What defines a successful Hybrid Clouds project?

362. Why do you do it?

363. What is the difference between % Complete and % work?

364. What defines a successful Hybrid Clouds project?

365. How should the information be delivered?

366. Goals for the Hybrid Clouds project. What is each stakeholders desired outcome for the Hybrid Clouds project?

367. What went right?

368. Who needs what information?

369. Which resources should be in the resource pool?

370. Who is allowed to perform which functions?

371. The list could probably go on, but, the thing that you would most like to know is, How long & How much?

372. Who will use the system?

373. What can you do to improve productivity?

374. What is the primary purpose of the human resource plan?

375. Changes based on input from stakeholders?

376. Why time management?

2.17 Activity Duration Estimates: Hybrid Clouds

377. Describe Hybrid Clouds project integration management in your own words. How does Hybrid Clouds project integration management relate to the Hybrid Clouds project life cycle, stakeholders, and the other Hybrid Clouds project management knowledge areas?

378. Are Hybrid Clouds project costs tracked in the general ledger?

379. What are the options you found to help people prepare for the exam?

380. Explanation notice how many choices are half right?

381. What are some crucial elements of a good Hybrid Clouds project plan?

382. What are two suggestions for ensuring adequate change control on Hybrid Clouds projects that involve outside contracts?

383. What is done after activity duration estimation?

384. What is the critical path for this Hybrid Clouds project and how long is it?

385. Who will provide training for the new application?

386. Calculate the expected duration for an activity that has a most likely time of 5, a pessimistic time of 13, and a optimiztic time of 3?

387. Are the causes of all variances identified?

388. Consider the history of modern quality management. How have experts such as Deming, Juran, Crosby, and Taguchi affected the quality movement and todays use of Six Sigma?

389. Do you think many other organizations could apply this methodology, or does each organization need to create its own methodology?

390. Are processes defined to monitor Hybrid Clouds project cost and schedule variances?

391. How do you enter durations, link tasks, and view critical path information?

392. Which frame seemed to be the most important and why?

393. Are activity dependencies identified?

394. How do functionality, system outputs, performance, reliability, and maintainability requirements affect quality planning?

395. Which best describes the relationship between standard deviation and risk?

2.18 Duration Estimating Worksheet: Hybrid Clouds

396. Science = process: remember the scientific method?

397. How can the Hybrid Clouds project be displayed graphically to better visualize the activities?

398. Is the Hybrid Clouds project responsive to community need?

399. Small or large Hybrid Clouds project?

400. What is your role?

401. What is cost and Hybrid Clouds project cost management?

402. When does your organization expect to be able to complete it?

403. Why estimate costs?

404. What utility impacts are there?

405. What is an Average Hybrid Clouds project?

406. What is next?

407. What questions do you have?

408. Does the Hybrid Clouds project provide

innovative ways for stakeholders to overcome obstacles or deliver better outcomes?

409. What work will be included in the Hybrid Clouds project?

410. Do any colleagues have experience with your organization and/or RFPs?

411. Will the Hybrid Clouds project collaborate with the local community and leverage resources?

2.19 Project Schedule: Hybrid Clouds

412. To what degree is do you feel the entire team was committed to the Hybrid Clouds project schedule?

413. Eliminate unnecessary activities. Are there activities that came from a template or previous Hybrid Clouds project that are not applicable on this phase of this Hybrid Clouds project?

414. How much slack is available in the Hybrid Clouds project?

415. Is Hybrid Clouds project work proceeding in accordance with the original Hybrid Clouds project schedule?

416. How detailed should a Hybrid Clouds project get?

417. Meet requirements?

418. Is infrastructure setup part of your Hybrid Clouds project?

419. Is the Hybrid Clouds project schedule available for all Hybrid Clouds project team members to review?

420. What is risk management?

421. Are you working on the right risks?

422. How can slack be negative?

423. How closely did the initial Hybrid Clouds project Schedule compare with the actual schedule?

424. Should you include sub-activities?

425. What is risk?

426. What documents, if any, will the subcontractor provide (eg Hybrid Clouds project schedule, quality plan etc)?

427. Change management required?

428. Are key risk mitigation strategies added to the Hybrid Clouds project schedule?

2.20 Cost Management Plan: Hybrid Clouds

429. Is a pmo (Hybrid Clouds project management office) in place and provide oversight to the Hybrid Clouds project?

430. Timeline and milestones?

431. Is there anything unique in this Hybrid Clouds projects scope statement that will affect resources?

432. Is Hybrid Clouds project status reviewed with the steering and executive teams at appropriate intervals?

433. Is a stakeholder management plan in place that covers topics?

434. Are there checklists created to determine if all quality processes are followed?

435. Does the Hybrid Clouds project have a Statement of Work?

436. Cost tracking and performance analysis – How will cost tracking and performance analysis be accomplished?

437. Contingency rundown curve be used on the Hybrid Clouds project?

438. Do all stakeholders know how to access this repository and where to find the Hybrid Clouds

project documentation?

439. Have the procedures for identifying budget variances been followed?

440. Has a Hybrid Clouds project Communications Plan been developed?

441. Is the quality assurance team identified?

442. Quality assurance overheads?

443. Ranged estimates?

444. Have all involved Hybrid Clouds project stakeholders and work groups committed to the Hybrid Clouds project?

445. Is there an issues management plan in place?

2.21 Activity Cost Estimates: Hybrid Clouds

446. In which phase of the acquisition process cycle does source qualifications reside?

447. One way to define activities is to consider how organization employees describe jobs to families and friends. You basically want to know, What do you do?

448. Can you delete activities or make them inactive?

449. How difficult will it be to do specific tasks on the Hybrid Clouds project?

450. How many activities should you have?

451. Does the activity use a common approach or business function to deliver its results?

452. Were the tasks or work products prepared by the consultant useful?

453. What is a Hybrid Clouds project Management Plan?

454. Does the activity serve a common type of customer?

455. How do you fund change orders?

456. If you are asked to lower your estimate because the price is too high, what are your options?

457. Was it performed on time?

458. Is costing method consistent with study goals?

459. What cost data should be used to estimate costs during the 2-year follow-up period?

460. Was the consultant knowledgeable about the program?

461. Measurable - are the targets measurable?

462. Estimated cost?

463. Is there anything unique in this Hybrid Clouds projects scope statement that will affect resources?

464. How and when do you enter into Hybrid Clouds project Procurement Management?

2.22 Cost Estimating Worksheet: Hybrid Clouds

465. What is the estimated labor cost today based upon this information?

466. What happens to any remaining funds not used?

467. What can be included?

468. Can a trend be established from historical performance data on the selected measure and are the criteria for using trend analysis or forecasting methods met?

469. What will others want?

470. Value pocket identification & quantification what are value pockets?

471. What is the purpose of estimating?

472. Is the Hybrid Clouds project responsive to community need?

473. Is it feasible to establish a control group arrangement?

474. Who is best positioned to know and assist in identifying corresponding factors?

475. What info is needed?

476. Does the Hybrid Clouds project provide innovative ways for stakeholders to overcome obstacles or deliver better outcomes?

477. How will the results be shared and to whom?

478. Ask: are others positioned to know, are others credible, and will others cooperate?

479. What additional Hybrid Clouds project(s) could be initiated as a result of this Hybrid Clouds project?

480. Will the Hybrid Clouds project collaborate with the local community and leverage resources?

481. Identify the timeframe necessary to monitor progress and collect data to determine how the selected measure has changed?

482. What costs are to be estimated?

2.23 Cost Baseline: Hybrid Clouds

483. Is there anything you need from upper management in order to be successful?

484. Have the resources used by the Hybrid Clouds project been reassigned to other units or Hybrid Clouds projects?

485. What is your organizations history in doing similar tasks?

486. Is there anything unique in this Hybrid Clouds projects scope statement that will affect resources?

487. Escalation criteria met?

488. How will cost estimates be used?

489. Definition of done can be traced back to the definitions of what are you providing to the customer in terms of deliverables?

490. Is the requested change request a result of changes in other Hybrid Clouds project(s)?

491. On time?

492. What is the consequence?

493. Has training and knowledge transfer of the operations organization been completed?

494. Should a more thorough impact analysis be

conducted?

495. Are you meeting with your team regularly?

496. Has the Hybrid Clouds project (or Hybrid Clouds project phase) been evaluated against each objective established in the product description and Integrated Hybrid Clouds project Plan?

497. How concrete were original objectives?

498. When should cost estimates be developed?

2.24 Quality Management Plan: Hybrid Clouds

499. Who is responsible for writing the qapp?

500. How will you know that a change is actually an improvement?

501. Was trending evident between reviews?

502. Account for the procedures used to verify the data quality of the data being reviewed?

503. How do you decide who is responsible for signing the data reports?

504. How are senior leaders, employees, and your organization involved in supporting the community?

505. How are calibration records kept?

506. How are training records kept?

507. Are you following the quality standards?

508. Is this a Requirement?

509. Does the program use modeling in the permitting or decision-making processes?

510. Is there a procedure for this process?

511. What other teams / processes would be impacted

by changes to the current process, and how?

512. What data do you gather/use/compile?

513. What are the appropriate test methods to be used?

514. What type of in-house testing do you conduct?

515. What is quality and how will you ensure it?

516. How do your action plans support the strategic objectives?

517. Is the steering committee active in Hybrid Clouds project oversight?

2.25 Quality Metrics: Hybrid Clouds

518. Were quality attributes reported?

519. Was material distributed on time?

520. What is the benchmark?

521. Is there alignment within your organization on definitions?

522. Did the team meet the Hybrid Clouds project success criteria documented in the Quality Metrics Matrix?

523. Were number of defects identified?

524. Are interface issues coordinated?

525. The metrics–what is being considered?

526. How do you calculate such metrics?

527. Should a modifier be included?

528. What happens if you get an abnormal result?

529. What metrics are important and most beneficial to measure?

530. Is material complete (and does it meet the standards)?

531. If the defect rate during testing is substantially

higher than that of the previous release (or a similar product), then ask: Did you plan for and actually improve testing effectiveness?

532. Can visual measures help you to filter visualizations of interest?

533. How does one achieve stability?

534. Can you correlate your quality metrics to profitability?

535. What documentation is required?

536. Are quality metrics defined?

2.26 Process Improvement Plan: Hybrid Clouds

537. Where are you now?

538. To elicit goal statements, do you ask a question such as, What do you want to achieve?

539. Modeling current processes is great, and will you ever see a return on that investment?

540. What personnel are the change agents for your initiative?

541. Where do you want to be?

542. What personnel are the champions for the initiative?

543. What personnel are the coaches for your initiative?

544. Has a process guide to collect the data been developed?

545. What makes people good SPI coaches?

546. Why quality management?

547. Are you making progress on your improvement plan?

548. Are you making progress on the goals?

549. Everyone agrees on what process improvement is, right?

550. How do you measure?

551. Are there forms and procedures to collect and record the data?

552. Does explicit definition of the measures exist?

553. Have storage and access mechanisms and procedures been determined?

554. Management commitment at all levels?

555. Why do you want to achieve the goal?

2.27 Responsibility Assignment Matrix: Hybrid Clouds

556. Identify potential or actual overruns and underruns?

557. Cwbs elements to be subcontracted, with identification of subcontractors?

558. Do others have the time to dedicate to your Hybrid Clouds project?

559. What happens when others get pulled for higher priority Hybrid Clouds projects?

560. Is all contract work included in the CWBS?

561. Are significant decision points, constraints, and interfaces identified as key milestones?

562. Are all authorized tasks assigned to identified organizational elements?

563. Which resource planning tool provides information on resource responsibility and accountability?

564. Does a missing responsibility indicate that the current Hybrid Clouds project is not yet fully understood?

565. Where does all this information come from?

566. Which Hybrid Clouds project management knowledge area is least mature?

567. All cwbs elements specified for external reporting?

568. How do you manage human resources?

569. Are people encouraged to bring up issues?

570. Are management actions taken to reduce indirect costs when there are significant adverse variances?

571. Are overhead costs budgets established on a basis consistent with anticipated direct business base?

572. Who is responsible for work and budgets for each wbs?

573. Too many is: do all the identified roles need to be routinely informed or only in exceptional circumstances?

2.28 Roles and Responsibilities: Hybrid Clouds

574. What expectations were met?

575. Key conclusions and recommendations: Are conclusions and recommendations relevant and acceptable?

576. Do the values and practices inherent in the culture of your organization foster or hinder the process?

577. Once the responsibilities are defined for the Hybrid Clouds project, have the deliverables, roles and responsibilities been clearly communicated to every participant?

578. Where are you most strong as a supervisor?

579. Are the quality assurance functions and related roles and responsibilities clearly defined?

580. Does your vision/mission support a culture of quality data?

581. Required skills, knowledge, experience?

582. What should you do now to prepare yourself for a promotion, increased responsibilities or a different job?

583. What should you highlight for improvement?

584. Who: who is involved?

585. Who is responsible for implementation activities and where will the functions, roles and responsibilities be defined?

586. What is working well?

587. Concern: where are you limited or have no authority, where you can not influence?

588. Was the expectation clearly communicated?

589. Implementation of actions: Who are the responsible units?

590. What should you do now to prepare for your career 5+ years from now?

591. Influence: what areas of organizational decision making are you able to influence when you do not have authority to make the final decision?

592. What are your major roles and responsibilities in the area of performance measurement and assessment?

2.29 Human Resource Management Plan: Hybrid Clouds

593. Are trade-offs between accepting the risk and mitigating the risk identified?

594. Are the quality tools and methods identified in the Quality Plan appropriate to the Hybrid Clouds project?

595. Is your organization primarily focused on a specific industry?

596. Hybrid Clouds project definition & scope?

597. Have all documents been archived in a Hybrid Clouds project repository for each release?

598. What communication items need improvement?

599. Are estimating assumptions and constraints captured?

600. Has the Hybrid Clouds project scope been baselined?

601. Are tasks tracked by hours?

602. Is there a formal process for updating the Hybrid Clouds project baseline?

603. Is it standard practice to formally commit stakeholders to the Hybrid Clouds project via

agreements?

604. Is there a set of procedures defining the scope, procedures, and deliverables defining quality control?

605. Do Hybrid Clouds project managers participating in the Hybrid Clouds project know the Hybrid Clouds projects true status first hand?

606. Have lessons learned been conducted after each Hybrid Clouds project release?

607. Account for the purpose of this Hybrid Clouds project by describing, at a high-level, what will be done. What is this Hybrid Clouds project aiming to achieve?

608. Are the appropriate IT resources adequate to meet planned commitments?

609. Does the Hybrid Clouds project have a Statement of Work?

2.30 Communications Management Plan: Hybrid Clouds

610. Who did you turn to if you had questions?

611. What is the stakeholders level of authority?

612. Are the stakeholders getting the information others need, are others consulted, are concerns addressed?

613. Who is the stakeholder?

614. Is there an important stakeholder who is actively opposed and will not receive messages?

615. Do you feel a register helps?

616. What steps can you take for a positive relationship?

617. Who have you worked with in past, similar initiatives?

618. Who needs to know and how much?

619. What are the interrelationships?

620. Are you constantly rushing from meeting to meeting?

621. What is the political influence?

622. What help do you and your team need from the stakeholder?

623. Conflict resolution -which method when?

624. What approaches to you feel are the best ones to use?

625. Who to learn from?

626. Who will use or be affected by the result of a Hybrid Clouds project?

627. Timing: when do the effects of the communication take place?

628. Will messages be directly related to the release strategy or phases of the Hybrid Clouds project?

2.31 Risk Management Plan: Hybrid Clouds

629. How is risk monitoring performed?

630. Are there alternative opinions/solutions/ processes you should explore?

631. Are the reports useful and easy to read?

632. What can you do to minimize the impact if it does?

633. Risk may be made during which step of risk management?

634. Why is product liability a serious issue?

635. Why do you want risk management?

636. User involvement: do you have the right users?

637. For software; are compilers and code generators available and suitable for the product to be built?

638. Are testing tools available and suitable?

639. Are formal technical reviews part of this process?

640. How is the audit profession changing?

641. Do benefits and chances of success outweigh potential damage if success is not attained?

642. Minimize cost and financial risk?

643. What is the likelihood that your organization would accept responsibility for the risk?

644. How much risk can you tolerate?

645. Are team members trained in the use of the tools?

646. What can go wrong?

647. What are it-specific requirements?

2.32 Risk Register: Hybrid Clouds

648. Are your objectives at risk?

649. What can be done about it?

650. Have other controls and solutions been implemented in other services which could be applied as an alternative to additional funding?

651. Market risk -will the new service or product be useful to your organization or marketable to others?

652. Preventative actions - planned actions to reduce the likelihood a risk will occur and/or reduce the seriousness should it occur. What should you do now?

653. What evidence do you have to justify the likelihood score of the risk (audit, incident report, claim, complaints, inspection, internal review)?

654. What is the appropriate level of risk management for this Hybrid Clouds project?

655. When would you develop a risk register?

656. Do you require further engagement?

657. What are your key risks/show istoppers and what is being done to manage them?

658. How could corresponding Risk affect the Hybrid Clouds project in terms of cost and schedule?

659. When will it happen?

660. How often will the Risk Management Plan and Risk Register be formally reviewed, and by whom?

661. Are there any knock-on effects/impact on any of the other areas?

662. What action, if any, has been taken to respond to the risk?

663. Who is accountable?

664. What risks might negatively or positively affect achieving the Hybrid Clouds project objectives?

665. What may happen or not go according to plan?

2.33 Probability and Impact Assessment: Hybrid Clouds

666. Do you have a mechanism for managing change?

667. Are the risk data complete?

668. Is there additional information that would make you more confident about your analysis?

669. Is the customer willing to participate in reviews?

670. What action do you usually take against risks?

671. What things are likely to change?

672. What is the past performance of the Hybrid Clouds project manager?

673. Do the people have the right combinations of skills?

674. Prioritized components/features?

675. Can this technology be absorbed with current level of expertise available in your organization?

676. Is the Hybrid Clouds project cutting across the entire organization?

677. What should be done with non-critical risks?

678. Are Hybrid Clouds project requirements stable?

679. How is the Hybrid Clouds project going to be managed?

680. How realistic is the timing of introduction?

681. Costs associated with late delivery or a defective product?

682. Do the requirements require the creation of new algorithms?

683. Do end-users have realistic expectations?

684. How are you working with risks?

685. Who should be notified of the occurrence of each of the risk indicators?

2.34 Probability and Impact Matrix: Hybrid Clouds

686. What needs to be DONE?

687. Should the risk be taken at all?

688. What has the Hybrid Clouds project manager forgotten to do?

689. What is the impact if the risk does occur?

690. Has the need for the Hybrid Clouds project been properly established?

691. Is the delay in one subHybrid Clouds project going to affect another?

692. Are Hybrid Clouds project requirements stable?

693. Who is going to be the consortium leader?

694. Several experts are offsite, and wish to be included. How can this be done?

695. Is the number of people on the Hybrid Clouds project team adequate to do the job?

696. Is there any sign of biased ranking?

697. How much risk do others need to take?

698. What risks were tracked?

699. What kind of preparation would be required to do this?

700. Who are the owners?

701. Who has experience with this?

2.35 Risk Data Sheet: Hybrid Clouds

702. What are you here for (Mission)?

703. How reliable is the data source?

704. What do people affected think about the need for, and practicality of preventive measures?

705. Has the most cost-effective solution been chosen?

706. What is the likelihood of it happening?

707. What are you trying to achieve (Objectives)?

708. What do you know?

709. How can hazards be reduced?

710. What can you do?

711. Type of risk identified?

712. Are new hazards created?

713. What if client refuses?

714. What are your core values?

715. How can it happen?

716. What can happen?

717. How do you handle product safely?

718. Do effective diagnostic tests exist?

719. Who has a vested interest in how you perform as your organization (our stakeholders)?

720. Is the data sufficiently specified in terms of the type of failure being analyzed, and its frequency or probability?

721. What is the environment within which you operate (social trends, economic, community values, broad based participation, national directions etc.)?

2.36 Procurement Management Plan: Hybrid Clouds

722. Does the Hybrid Clouds project have a Statement of Work?

723. Is there a procurement management plan in place?

724. Does the business case include how the Hybrid Clouds project aligns with your organizations strategic goals & objectives?

725. Similar Hybrid Clouds projects?

726. Is Hybrid Clouds project work proceeding in accordance with the original Hybrid Clouds project schedule?

727. Are the budget estimates reasonable?

728. Was your organizations estimating methodology being used and followed?

729. Have key stakeholders been identified?

730. Are governance roles and responsibilities documented?

731. Is it possible to track all classes of Hybrid Clouds project work (e.g. scheduled, un-scheduled, defect repair, etc.)?

732. Are the key elements of a Hybrid Clouds project Charter present?

733. Is there an approved case?

734. Is the assigned Hybrid Clouds project manager a PMP (Certified Hybrid Clouds project manager) and experienced?

735. Is the Hybrid Clouds project schedule available for all Hybrid Clouds project team members to review?

736. Is the schedule updated on a periodic basis?

737. Are issues raised, assessed, actioned, and resolved in a timely and efficient manner?

2.37 Source Selection Criteria: Hybrid Clouds

738. What are the guidelines regarding award without considerations?

739. What common questions or problems are associated with debriefings?

740. How will you decide an evaluators write up is sufficient?

741. What is price analysis and when should it be performed?

742. What management structure does your organization consider as optimal for performing the contract?

743. Is the contracting office likely to receive more purchase requests for this item or service during the coming year?

744. What does an evaluation address and what does a sample resemble?

745. How important is cost in the source selection decision relative to past performance and technical considerations?

746. What are open book debriefings?

747. What information may not be provided?

748. Do you want to wait until all offerors have been evaluated?

749. How should comments received in response to a RFP be handled?

750. Why promote competition?

751. What should a DRFP include?

752. What documentation is needed for a tradeoff decision?

753. What is cost analysis and when should it be performed?

754. Does an evaluation need to include the identification of strengths and weaknesses?

755. How much weight should be placed on past performance information?

756. What is the role of counsel in the procurement process?

2.38 Stakeholder Management Plan: Hybrid Clouds

757. Is it standard practice to formally commit stakeholders to the Hybrid Clouds project via agreements?

758. Does a documented Hybrid Clouds project organizational policy & plan (i.e. governance model) exist?

759. What is to be the method of release?

760. Will all relevant stakeholders be included within the review process?

761. After observing execution of process, is it in compliance with the documented Plan?

762. Are there nonconformance issues?

763. How is information analyzed, and what specific pieces of data would be of interest to the Hybrid Clouds project manager?

764. Have all unresolved risks been documented?

765. What is the primary function of the Activity Decomposition Decision Tree?

766. Are there standards for code development?

767. Is pert / critical path or equivalent methodology

being used?

768. Are all payments made according to the contract(s)?

769. Is quality monitored from the perspective of the customers needs and expectations?

770. Why would you develop a Hybrid Clouds project Business Plan?

771. Does the Hybrid Clouds project have a formal Hybrid Clouds project Charter?

772. Do you know what your customers expectations are regarding this process?

2.39 Change Management Plan: Hybrid Clouds

773. Change invariability confront many relationships especially the already stated that require a set of behaviours What roles with in your organization are affected and how?

774. Will the culture embrace or reject this change?

775. What provokes organizational change?

776. What risks may occur upfront, during implementation and after implementation?

777. Do you need a new organizational structure?

778. What method and medium would you use to announce a message?

779. What prerequisite knowledge or training is required?

780. What work practices will be affected?

781. Has a training need analysis been carried out?

782. Will the readiness criteria be met prior to the training roll out?

783. Who will do the training?

784. Who will be the change levers?

785. Will a different work structure focus people on what is important?

786. What risks may occur upfront?

787. Identify the current level of skills and knowledge and behaviours of the group that will be impacted on. What prerequisite knowledge do corresponding groups need?

788. Are there any restrictions on who can receive the communications?

789. What prerequisite knowledge do corresponding groups need?

790. Do you need new systems?

791. Has the training provider been established?

3.0 Executing Process Group: Hybrid Clouds

792. What were things that you need to improve?

793. Why should Hybrid Clouds project managers strive to make jobs look easy?

794. What type of information goes in the quality assurance plan?

795. How does the job market and current state of the economy affect human resource management?

796. When is the appropriate time to bring the scorecard to Board meetings?

797. Will additional funds be needed for hardware or software?

798. How will you avoid scope creep?

799. Is activity definition the first process involved in Hybrid Clouds project time management?

800. How many different communication channels does the Hybrid Clouds project team have?

801. What is the product of your Hybrid Clouds project?

802. What are the critical steps involved with strategy mapping?

803. Are decisions made in a timely manner?

804. What are deliverables of your Hybrid Clouds project?

805. How could you control progress of your Hybrid Clouds project?

806. Were sponsors and decision makers available when needed outside regularly scheduled meetings?

807. When will the Hybrid Clouds project be done?

808. What is the difference between conceptual, application, and evaluative questions?

809. What are some crucial elements of a good Hybrid Clouds project plan?

810. What type of people would you want on your team?

811. Do Hybrid Clouds project managers understand your organizational context for Hybrid Clouds projects?

3.1 Team Member Status Report: Hybrid Clouds

812. Does your organization have the means (staff, money, contract, etc.) to produce or to acquire the product, good, or service?

813. Are your organizations Hybrid Clouds projects more successful over time?

814. Is there evidence that staff is taking a more professional approach toward management of your organizations Hybrid Clouds projects?

815. When a teams productivity and success depend on collaboration and the efficient flow of information, what generally fails them?

816. Does the product, good, or service already exist within your organization?

817. What specific interest groups do you have in place?

818. Are the products of your organizations Hybrid Clouds projects meeting customers objectives?

819. How does this product, good, or service meet the needs of the Hybrid Clouds project and your organization as a whole?

820. How much risk is involved?

821. Do you have an Enterprise Hybrid Clouds project Management Office (EPMO)?

822. The problem with Reward & Recognition Programs is that the truly deserving people all too often get left out. How can you make it practical?

823. Does every department have to have a Hybrid Clouds project Manager on staff?

824. Are the attitudes of staff regarding Hybrid Clouds project work improving?

825. How can you make it practical?

826. What is to be done?

827. How it is to be done?

828. How will resource planning be done?

829. Will the staff do training or is that done by a third party?

830. Why is it to be done?

3.2 Change Request: Hybrid Clouds

831. How is quality being addressed on the Hybrid Clouds project?

832. Have scm procedures for noting the change, recording it, and reporting it been followed?

833. How many lines of code must be changed to implement the change?

834. Since there are no change requests in your Hybrid Clouds project at this point, what must you have before you begin?

835. How shall the implementation of changes be recorded?

836. Are there requirements attributes that can discriminate between high and low reliability?

837. What is the function of the change control committee?

838. How well do experienced software developers predict software change?

839. Change request coordination ?

840. Where do changes come from?

841. Will there be a change request form in use?

842. Describe how modifications, enhancements,

defects and/or deficiencies shall be notified (e.g. Problem Reports, Change Requests etc) and managed. Detail warranty and/or maintenance periods?

843. How can changes be graded?

844. Who has responsibility for approving and ranking changes?

845. What mechanism is used to appraise others of changes that are made?

846. Customer acceptance plan how will the customer verify the change has been implemented successfully?

847. Who is responsible to authorize changes?

848. How is the change documented (format, content, storage)?

849. Who is communicating the change?

850. Have all related configuration items been properly updated?

3.3 Change Log: Hybrid Clouds

851. Who initiated the change request?

852. Is the requested change request a result of changes in other Hybrid Clouds project(s)?

853. Do the described changes impact on the integrity or security of the system?

854. When was the request submitted?

855. Is the change backward compatible without limitations?

856. Is the change request open, closed or pending?

857. How does this change affect scope?

858. How does this relate to the standards developed for specific business processes?

859. Is the submitted change a new change or a modification of a previously approved change?

860. Will the Hybrid Clouds project fail if the change request is not executed?

861. How does this change affect the timeline of the schedule?

862. Is the change request within Hybrid Clouds project scope?

863. Does the suggested change request represent a desired enhancement to the products functionality?

864. When was the request approved?

865. Is this a mandatory replacement?

866. Does the suggested change request seem to represent a necessary enhancement to the product?

3.4 Decision Log: Hybrid Clouds

867. At what point in time does loss become unacceptable?

868. How do you define success?

869. What are the cost implications?

870. Linked to original objective?

871. What is your overall strategy for quality control / quality assurance procedures?

872. Is everything working as expected?

873. It becomes critical to track and periodically revisit both operational effectiveness; Are you noticing all that you need to, and are you interpreting what you see effectively?

874. How consolidated and comprehensive a story can you tell by capturing currently available incident data in a central location and through a log of key decisions during an incident?

875. How does the use a Decision Support System influence the strategies/tactics or costs?

876. Does anything need to be adjusted?

877. What makes you different or better than others companies selling the same thing?

878. What was the rationale for the decision?

879. How does an increasing emphasis on cost containment influence the strategies and tactics used?

880. Behaviors; what are guidelines that the team has identified that will assist them with getting the most out of team meetings?

881. Is your opponent open to a non-traditional workflow, or will it likely challenge anything you do?

882. Do strategies and tactics aimed at less than full control reduce the costs of management or simply shift the cost burden?

883. Who will be given a copy of this document and where will it be kept?

884. Which variables make a critical difference?

885. How effective is maintaining the log at facilitating organizational learning?

886. Decision-making process; how will the team make decisions?

3.5 Quality Audit: Hybrid Clouds

887. How does your organization know that its Governance system is appropriately effective and constructive?

888. Statements of intent remain exactly that until they are put into effect. The next step is to deploy the already stated intentions. In other words, do the plans happen in reality?

889. Is there a written corporate quality policy?

890. How does your organization ensure that equipment is appropriately maintained and producing valid results?

891. What does an analysis of your organizations staff profile suggest in terms of its planning, and how is this being addressed?

892. What are you trying to accomplish with this audit?

893. Are training programs documented?

894. Does the supplier use a formal quality system?

895. How does your organization know that its relationships with other relevant organizations are appropriately effective and constructive?

896. How does your organization know that its relationship with its (past) staff is appropriately

effective and constructive?

897. Do the suppliers use a formal quality system?

898. How does your organization know that its relationships with the community at large are appropriately effective and constructive?

899. How does your organization know that its system for managing intellectual property issues is appropriately effective, constructive and fair?

900. Are all areas associated with the storage and reconditioning of devices clean, free of rubbish, adequately ventilated and in good repair?

901. How does your organization know that the support for its staff is appropriately effective and constructive?

902. Is your organizational structure established and each positions responsibility defined?

903. Does the suppliers quality system have a written procedure for corrective action when a defect occurs?

904. How does the organization know that its system for maintaining and advancing the capabilities of its staff, particularly in relation to the Mission of the organization, is appropriately effective and constructive?

905. How does your organization know that its general support services planning and management systems are appropriately effective and constructive?

906. Does the audit organization have experience in performing the required work for entities of your type and size?

3.6 Team Directory: Hybrid Clouds

907. Contract requirements complied with?

908. Why is the work necessary?

909. Who will talk to the customer?

910. Process decisions: are contractors adequately prosecuting the work?

911. How will you accomplish and manage the objectives?

912. When will you produce deliverables?

913. Process decisions: is work progressing on schedule and per contract requirements?

914. Who are your stakeholders (customers, sponsors, end users, team members)?

915. Is construction on schedule?

916. Decisions: is the most suitable form of contract being used?

917. Where should the information be distributed?

918. Days from the time the issue is identified?

919. Does a Hybrid Clouds project team directory list all resources assigned to the Hybrid Clouds project?

920. Do purchase specifications and configurations match requirements?

921. Who should receive information (all stakeholders)?

922. Who are the Team Members?

923. How and in what format should information be presented?

924. Who will write the meeting minutes and distribute?

925. When does information need to be distributed?

3.7 Team Operating Agreement: Hybrid Clouds

926. Do you call or email participants to ensure understanding, follow-through and commitment to the meeting outcomes?

927. What are the boundaries (organizational or geographic) within which you operate?

928. Are there differences in access to communication and collaboration technology based on team member location?

929. What types of accommodations will be formulated and put in place for sustaining the team?

930. How will group handle unplanned absences?

931. What is teaming?

932. Are there more than two functional areas represented by your team?

933. What is the number of cases currently teamed?

934. What are the safety issues/risks that need to be addressed and/or that the team needs to consider?

935. Do you ask participants to close laptops and place mobile devices on silent on the table while the meeting is in progress?

936. Do you post any action items, due dates, and responsibilities on the team website?

937. Do you ensure that all participants know how to use the required technology?

938. Do you begin with a question to engage everyone?

939. Reimbursements: how will the team members be reimbursed for expenses and time commitments?

940. Must your team members rely on the expertise of other members to complete tasks?

941. How does teaming fit in with overall organizational goals and meet organizational needs?

942. What is your unique contribution to your organization?

943. What are some potential sources of conflict among team members?

944. To whom do you deliver your services?

945. Do team members reside in more than two countries?

3.8 Team Performance Assessment: Hybrid Clouds

946. To what degree do members articulate the goals beyond the team membership?

947. To what degree can the team measure progress against specific goals?

948. To what degree will the team adopt a concrete, clearly understood, and agreed-upon approach that will result in achievement of the teams goals?

949. If you have criticized someones work for method variance in your role as reviewer, what was the circumstance?

950. Which situations call for a more extreme type of adaptiveness in which team members actually re-define roles?

951. What do you think is the most constructive thing that could be done now to resolve considerations and disputes about method variance?

952. How do you keep key people outside the group informed about its accomplishments?

953. To what degree does the teams purpose contain themes that are particularly meaningful and memorable?

954. To what degree can the team ensure that all

members are individually and jointly accountable for the teams purpose, goals, approach, and work-products?

955. To what degree do all members feel responsible for all agreed-upon measures?

956. Where to from here?

957. Individual task proficiency and team process behavior: what is important for team functioning?

958. To what degree are corresponding categories of skills either actually or potentially represented across the membership?

959. What are teams?

960. What makes opportunities more or less obvious?

961. Social categorization and intergroup behaviour: Does minimal intergroup discrimination make social identity more positive?

962. To what degree can team members meet frequently enough to accomplish the teams ends?

963. When a reviewer complains about method variance, what is the essence of the complaint?

964. To what degree does the teams work approach provide opportunity for members to engage in fact-based problem solving?

965. Do friends perform better than acquaintances?

3.9 Team Member Performance Assessment: Hybrid Clouds

966. In what areas would you like to concentrate your knowledge and resources?

967. What does collaboration look like?

968. Are any validation activities performed?

969. What are the evaluation strategies (e.g., reaction, learning, behavior, results) used. What evaluation results did you have?

970. What evaluation results did you have?

971. Verify business objectives. Are they appropriate, and well-articulated?

972. Should a ratee get a copy of all the raters documents about the employees performance?

973. What, if any, steps are available for employees who feel they have been unfairly or inaccurately rated?

974. Do the goals support your organizations goals?

975. How often are assessments to be conducted?

976. How are assessments designed, delivered, and otherwise used to maximize training?

977. What changes do you need to make to align practices with beliefs?

978. Goals met?

979. To what degree does the teams approach to its work allow for modification and improvement over time?

980. How do you implement Cost Reduction?

981. How do you determine which data are the most important to use, analyze, or review?

982. Did training work?

983. How is assessment information achieved, stored?

984. What is a general description of the processes under performance measurement and assessment?

3.10 Issue Log: Hybrid Clouds

985. Can an impact cause deviation beyond team, stage or Hybrid Clouds project tolerances?

986. Are the Hybrid Clouds project issues uniquely identified, including to which product they refer?

987. Why not more evaluators?

988. Are they needed?

989. Which team member will work with each stakeholder?

990. Which stakeholders are thought leaders, influences, or early adopters?

991. Do you prepare stakeholder engagement plans?

992. Who do you turn to if you have questions?

993. How much time does it take to do it?

994. Are there too many who have an interest in some aspect of your work?

995. What help do you and your team need from the stakeholders?

996. Is access to the Issue Log controlled?

997. Persistence; will users learn a work around or will they be bothered every time?

998. What is the impact on the risks?

999. Who is the issue assigned to?

1000. What approaches do you use?

1001. What date was the issue resolved?

1002. How is this initiative related to other portfolios, programs, or Hybrid Clouds projects?

4.0 Monitoring and Controlling Process Group: Hybrid Clouds

1003. What resources are necessary?

1004. How will staff learn how to use the deliverables?

1005. How was the program set-up initiated?

1006. How is agile Hybrid Clouds project management done?

1007. How well defined and documented were the Hybrid Clouds project management processes you chose to use?

1008. Contingency planning. if a risk event occurs, what will you do?

1009. What are the deliverables?

1010. Who are the Hybrid Clouds project stakeholders?

1011. How can you monitor progress?

1012. Is the program in place as intended?

1013. What are the goals of the program?

1014. What factors are contributing to progress or delay in the achievement of products and results?

1015. What is the timeline?

1016. Does the solution fit in with organizations technical architectural requirements?

1017. Key stakeholders to work with. How many potential communications channels exist on the Hybrid Clouds project?

1018. Feasibility: how much money, time, and effort can you put into this?

1019. Is it what was agreed upon?

1020. How well did you do?

1021. Is there sufficient time allotted between the general system design and the detailed system design phases?

4.1 Project Performance Report: Hybrid Clouds

1022. How is the data used?

1023. How will procurement be coordinated with other Hybrid Clouds project aspects, such as scheduling and performance reporting?

1024. To what degree are sub-teams possible or necessary?

1025. To what degree does the team possess adequate membership to achieve its ends?

1026. To what degree is the information network consistent with the structure of the formal organization?

1027. To what degree do team members frequently explore the teams purpose and its implications?

1028. To what degree does the teams work approach provide opportunity for members to engage in results-based evaluation?

1029. To what degree are the skill areas critical to team performance present?

1030. To what degree are the demands of the task compatible with and converge with the mission and functions of the formal organization?

1031. Next Steps?

1032. To what degree will the approach capitalize on and enhance the skills of all team members in a manner that takes into consideration other demands on members of the team?

1033. To what degree can all members engage in open and interactive considerations?

1034. To what degree does the teams work approach provide opportunity for members to engage in open interaction?

1035. To what degree are fresh input and perspectives systematically caught and added (for example, through information and analysis, new members, and senior sponsors)?

1036. To what degree does the information network provide individuals with the information they require?

1037. To what degree do the relationships of the informal organization motivate taskrelevant behavior and facilitate task completion?

1038. To what degree can the cognitive capacity of individuals accommodate the flow of information?

1039. To what degree do team members feel that the purpose of the team is important, if not exciting?

4.2 Variance Analysis: Hybrid Clouds

1040. Are estimates of costs at completion generated in a rational, consistent manner?

1041. Are there knowledgeable Hybrid Clouds projections of future performance?

1042. Favorable or unfavorable variance?

1043. What is the budgeted cost for work scheduled?

1044. Can the contractor substantiate work package and planning package budgets?

1045. There are detailed schedules which support control account and work package start and completion dates/events?

1046. What business event causes fluctuations?

1047. Are authorized changes being incorporated in a timely manner?

1048. What is exceptional?

1049. Who are responsible for overhead performance control of related costs?

1050. How have the setting and use of standards changed over time?

1051. Are there quarterly budgets with quarterly performance comparisons?

1052. Are meaningful indicators identified for use in measuring the status of cost and schedule performance?

1053. How does your organization measure performance?

1054. Are overhead costs budgets established on a basis consistent with the anticipated direct business base?

1055. Does the accounting system provide a basis for auditing records of direct costs chargeable to the contract?

1056. What are the direct labor dollars and/or hours?

1057. Budgeted cost for work performed?

1058. Are there changes in the direct base to which overhead costs are allocated?

1059. Are data elements reconcilable between internal summary reports and reports forwarded to the stakeholders?

4.3 Earned Value Status: Hybrid Clouds

1060. Earned value can be used in almost any Hybrid Clouds project situation and in almost any Hybrid Clouds project environment. it may be used on large Hybrid Clouds projects, medium sized Hybrid Clouds projects, tiny Hybrid Clouds projects (in cut-down form), complex and simple Hybrid Clouds projects and in any market sector. some people, of course, know all about earned value, they have used it for years - but perhaps not as effectively as they could have?

1061. How does this compare with other Hybrid Clouds projects?

1062. How much is it going to cost by the finish?

1063. If earned value management (EVM) is so good in determining the true status of a Hybrid Clouds project and Hybrid Clouds project its completion, why is it that hardly any one uses it in information systems related Hybrid Clouds projects?

1064. Verification is a process of ensuring that the developed system satisfies the stakeholders agreements and specifications; Are you building the product right? What do you verify?

1065. What is the unit of forecast value?

1066. Where are your problem areas?

1067. Where is evidence-based earned value in your organization reported?

1068. When is it going to finish?

1069. Are you hitting your Hybrid Clouds projects targets?

1070. Validation is a process of ensuring that the developed system will actually achieve the stakeholders desired outcomes; Are you building the right product? What do you validate?

4.4 Risk Audit: Hybrid Clouds

1071. Are you aware of the industry standards that apply to your operations?

1072. Do you promote education and training opportunities?

1073. Strategic business risk audit methodologies; are corresponding an attempt to sell other services, and is management becoming the client of the audit rather than the shareholder?

1074. Are auditors able to effectively apply more soft evidence found in the risk-assessment process with the results of more tangible audit evidence found through more substantive testing?

1075. What impact does prior experience have on decisions made during the risk-assessment process?

1076. What does monitoring consist of?

1077. Will safety checks of personal equipment supplied by competitors be conducted?

1078. What impact does experience with one client have on decisions made for other clients during the risk-assessment process?

1079. Estimated size of product in number of programs, files, transactions?

1080. Do requirements demand the use of new

analysis, design, or testing methods?

1081. Why do audits fail?

1082. Improving fraud detection: do auditors react to abnormal inconsistencies between financial and non-financial measures?

1083. Do you have an emergency plan?

1084. Who is responsible for what?

1085. Does your organization have an up-to-date constitution?

1086. Do requirements put excessive performance constraints on the product?

1087. What resources are needed to achieve program results?

1088. Are requirements fully understood by the team and customers?

1089. Are all programs planned and conducted according to recognized safety standards?

1090. Is safety information provided to all involved?

4.5 Contractor Status Report: Hybrid Clouds

1091. Describe how often regular updates are made to the proposed solution. Are corresponding regular updates included in the standard maintenance plan?

1092. If applicable; describe your standard schedule for new software version releases. Are new software version releases included in the standard maintenance plan?

1093. What process manages the contracts?

1094. Who can list a Hybrid Clouds project as organization experience, your organization or a previous employee of your organization?

1095. How does the proposed individual meet each requirement?

1096. What was the final actual cost?

1097. How long have you been using the services?

1098. What are the minimum and optimal bandwidth requirements for the proposed solution?

1099. What was the overall budget or estimated cost?

1100. What is the average response time for answering a support call?

1101. What was the actual budget or estimated cost for your organizations services?

1102. How is risk transferred?

1103. What was the budget or estimated cost for your organizations services?

1104. Are there contractual transfer concerns?

4.6 Formal Acceptance: Hybrid Clouds

1105. What features, practices, and processes proved to be strengths or weaknesses?

1106. What can you do better next time?

1107. Did the Hybrid Clouds project manager and team act in a professional and ethical manner?

1108. Was business value realized?

1109. Who supplies data?

1110. Was the Hybrid Clouds project goal achieved?

1111. General estimate of the costs and times to complete the Hybrid Clouds project?

1112. Was the sponsor/customer satisfied?

1113. What function(s) does it fill or meet?

1114. Does it do what client said it would?

1115. Who would use it?

1116. Is formal acceptance of the Hybrid Clouds project product documented and distributed?

1117. Was the Hybrid Clouds project work done on time, within budget, and according to specification?

1118. Was the Hybrid Clouds project managed well?

1119. What was done right?

1120. Did the Hybrid Clouds project achieve its MOV?

1121. Was the client satisfied with the Hybrid Clouds project results?

1122. How well did the team follow the methodology?

1123. How does your team plan to obtain formal acceptance on your Hybrid Clouds project?

1124. Do you perform formal acceptance or burn-in tests?

5.0 Closing Process Group: Hybrid Clouds

1125. Is the Hybrid Clouds project funded?

1126. What were the actual outcomes?

1127. If a risk event occurs, what will you do?

1128. Is the Hybrid Clouds project funded?

1129. What will you do?

1130. How will you do it?

1131. What is the Hybrid Clouds project name and date of completion?

1132. Specific - is the objective clear in terms of what, how, when, and where the situation will be changed?

1133. What were things that you did very well and want to do the same again on the next Hybrid Clouds project?

1134. Did the Hybrid Clouds project team have the right skills?

1135. Was the schedule met?

1136. What were the desired outcomes?

1137. What is the risk of failure to your organization?

1138. What is an Encumbrance?

1139. What do you need to do?

1140. Did you do what you said you were going to do?

1141. What can you do better next time, and what specific actions can you take to improve?

5.1 Procurement Audit: Hybrid Clouds

1142. Has your organization fulfilled its obligations related to the payment of social security contributions and taxes?

1143. In case of time and material and labour hour contracts, does surveillance give an adequate and reasonable assurance that the contractor is using efficient methods and effective cost controls?

1144. Are there systems for recording and monitoring in order to discover malpractice and fraud in the procurement function/unit?

1145. Are there policies regarding special approval for capital expenditures?

1146. Audits: when was your last independent public accountant (ipa) audit and what were the results?

1147. Did your organization identify the full contract value and include options and provisions for renewals?

1148. How is the evaluation of contract performance organized?

1149. If the expert was allowed to submit a tender, was all the relevant information the expert had gained from his earlier involvement made available to the other bidders?

1150. Is there no evidence of collusion between

bidders?

1151. Is a cash flow chart prepared and used in determining the timing and term of investments?

1152. Could bidders learn all relevant information straight from the tender documents?

1153. Where funding is being arranged by borrowings, do corresponding have the necessary approval and legal authority?

1154. Is there no evidence of favouritism towards a particular contractor during the evaluation and negotiation processes?

1155. Are receiving reports on file for all claims for equipment, supplies and materials in the paid claims file?

1156. When tenders were actually rejected because they were abnormally low, were reasons for this decision given and were they sufficiently grounded?

1157. Have guidelines incorporating the principles and objectives of a robust procurement practice been established?

1158. Do contracts contain regular reviews, targets and quality standards in order to assess suppliers performance?

1159. Are there regular reviews and analysis of the performance of the procurement function/unit?

1160. Are the number of checking accounts where

cash segregation is not required kept to a reasonable number?

1161. Does your organization have an administrative timetable to assist the staff in implementing the budget calendar?

5.2 Contract Close-Out: Hybrid Clouds

1162. Are the signers the authorized officials?

1163. Was the contract type appropriate?

1164. How does it work?

1165. Parties: who is involved?

1166. What is capture management?

1167. Change in knowledge?

1168. Was the contract sufficiently clear so as not to result in numerous disputes and misunderstandings?

1169. Parties: Authorized?

1170. How is the contracting office notified of the automatic contract close-out?

1171. Has each contract been audited to verify acceptance and delivery?

1172. Have all acceptance criteria been met prior to final payment to contractors?

1173. Have all contract records been included in the Hybrid Clouds project archives?

1174. Change in attitude or behavior?

1175. What happens to the recipient of services?

1176. Change in circumstances?

1177. How/when used ?

1178. Have all contracts been closed?

1179. Have all contracts been completed?

1180. Was the contract complete without requiring numerous changes and revisions?

5.3 Project or Phase Close-Out: Hybrid Clouds

1181. What hierarchical authority does the stakeholder have in your organization?

1182. Does the lesson describe a function that would be done differently the next time?

1183. What security considerations needed to be addressed during the procurement life cycle?

1184. What process was planned for managing issues/ risks?

1185. Was the user/client satisfied with the end product?

1186. Planned remaining costs?

1187. Who controlled the resources for the Hybrid Clouds project?

1188. Who controlled key decisions that were made?

1189. What went well?

1190. When and how were information needs best met?

1191. How much influence did the stakeholder have over others?

1192. Does the lesson educate others to improve performance?

1193. What benefits or impacts does the stakeholder group expect to obtain as a result of the Hybrid Clouds project?

1194. Who exerted influence that has positively affected or negatively impacted the Hybrid Clouds project?

1195. What advantages do the an individual interview have over a group meeting, and vice-versa?

1196. Which changes might a stakeholder be required to make as a result of the Hybrid Clouds project?

1197. What is a Risk Management Process?

1198. What are the mandatory communication needs for each stakeholder?

5.4 Lessons Learned: Hybrid Clouds

1199. How many interest groups are stakeholders?

1200. How useful and complete was the Hybrid Clouds project document repository?

1201. How well prepared were you to receive Hybrid Clouds project deliverables?

1202. How was the Hybrid Clouds project controlled?

1203. Are lessons learned documented?

1204. What are the expectations of the individuals?

1205. How efficient and effective were Hybrid Clouds project team meetings?

1206. Why does your organization need a lessons learned (LL) capability?

1207. Who managed most of the communication within the Hybrid Clouds project?

1208. What Hybrid Clouds project circumstances were not anticipated?

1209. How effective were Hybrid Clouds project audits?

1210. Are you in full regulatory compliance?

1211. Did the team work well together?

1212. How well did the Hybrid Clouds project Manager respond to questions or comments related to the Hybrid Clouds project?

1213. What needs to be done over or differently?

1214. What did you do right?

1215. What is the supplier dependency?

1216. How accurately and timely was the Risk Management Log updated or reviewed?

1217. Under what legal authority did your organization head and program manager direct your organization and Hybrid Clouds project?

1218. How adequately involved did you feel in Hybrid Clouds project decisions?

Index

resolved 202, 231

resource 3-4, 116, 131, 149, 151, 155, 160-162, 183, 187, 209, 212

resources 2, 7, 22, 24-25, 32, 36, 56, 68, 85, 92, 95, 105, 109, 116, 120, 125, 138, 150-152, 154, 158, 161, 166, 169, 172, 174-175, 184, 188, 222, 228, 232, 241, 253

respect 1

respond 194, 256

responded 11

response 23-24, 93-94, 96-97, 204, 242

responses 80

responsive 165, 173

restrict 139

result 62, 82, 142, 174-175, 179, 190, 215, 226, 251, 254

resulted 98

resulting 61

results 8, 28, 31, 69, 74, 78, 81, 86-87, 95, 98, 131-132, 149, 154, 171, 174, 219, 228, 232, 240-241, 245, 248

Retain 102

retained 67

retention 48

retrospect 111

return 82, 159, 181

revenue 25, 55

revenues 49

review 9, 132, 159, 167, 193, 202, 205, 229

reviewed 38, 143, 169, 177, 194, 256

reviewer 226-227

reviews 149-150, 158, 177, 191, 195, 249

revised 59, 98

revisions 252

revisit 217

reward 47, 53, 71, 212

rewarded 25

rewards 100

rework 48

rights 1

robust 249

routine 94

routinely 184

rubbish 220

rundown 169

rushing 189

9 780655 842699